Good Business Communication

Doris Wheatley has spent her life in Cambridge. Born in 1915, she was educated at the Perse Girls' School and Girton College, where she became Director of Studies in Archaeology and Anthropology. In 1966 she left the academic world to join a company, Cambridge Consultants (Training) Ltd. She became Managing Director in 1970 and eventually sole owner of the company which she re-named Cambridge Communication as she decided this better described its activities. Her client list was once described as 'a roll-call of British industry'. She sold the company in 1984, although she continues to work as a freelance communication consultant.

Doris Wheatley was married and has a twin son and daughter.

SERIES EDITORS: Stephen Coote and Bryan Loughrey

Good Business Communication

Doris Wheatley

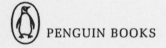 PENGUIN BOOKS

PENGUIN BOOKS

Published by the Penguin Group
27 Wrights Lane, London W8 5TZ, England
Viking Penguin Inc., 40 West 23rd Street, New York, New York 10010, USA
Penguin Books Australia Ltd, Ringwood, Victoria, Australia
Penguin Books Canada Ltd, 2801 John Street, Markham, Ontario, Canada L3R 1B4
Penguin Books (NZ) Ltd, 182–190 Wairau Road, Auckland 10, New Zealand

Penguin Books Ltd, Registered Offices: Harmondsworth, Middlesex, England

First published 1988

Filmset in Linotron 202 Melior

Typeset, printed and bound in Great Britain by
Hazell Watson & Viney Limited
Member of BPCC plc
Aylesbury Bucks

For Kay and Muriel,
without whose unfailing help
this book would have been much worse

Contents

Preface

To be born with a silver spoon in one's mouth is the best start to a successful life, we used to be told. Alas, I was born with only a piece of chalk in my hand. In 1915, when this event took place, chalk boards were the most common visual aids. Therefore I was destined to become a teacher, and this I have been for fifty of my seventy-three years. I have taught people of all ages, from nursery-school children to the eighty-year-olds and over who came to my adult education classes. I owe a particular debt to the Workers' Educational Association for which organization I worked for many years. I learnt there that if I didn't 'get the message across' in the first week, no one would be there in the second. It was a hard school, but a most valuable one. I also taught in the Faculty of Archaeology and Anthropology in Cambridge University for many years. There I acquired, I am told, a peculiar reputation for somehow helping potential rugby and rowing blues to pass their Tripos examinations.

When, almost at the age of fifty-one, I left what the journalists have called 'the groves of Academe' to join the hard world of business, I knew a very great deal about teaching and its corollary, learning, and absolutely nothing about business. Again, I learnt the hard way. At the beginning of my business life, when working for the Engineering Industry Training Board (which still remains one of the most exciting jobs I have ever done), I walked into a factory with a notebook and pen and started to ask questions about what the shop-floor workers were doing. I found myself facing angry shop stewards. No one but an industry ignoramus or a lunatic would have done what I did. I hope I was an ignoramus.

The company I joined – quite fortuitously, because I met one of the directors and started arguing with him – was Cambridge Consultants (Training) Limited. It didn't take long to discover that this company was doing what I had been doing for so long: structuring learning. The reason why the rowing and rugby men managed to get their degrees was because I had so structured their learning that they

achieved the maximum result in the minimum time. It is not necessary, I hope, to point out that this was not a suitable beginning to
an *academic* career, but it was the best way to acquire sufficient
information for a particular purpose – in this case, acquiring a
degree. This is what a great deal of communication in business is
about.

After many years, Cambridge Consultants (Training) Limited
decided that, as part of its activities was concerned with doing without training and all of it with communication, its name should be
changed to Cambridge Communication Limited.

To me, what I was doing in teaching small children, older children, undergraduates, all-age members of adult education classes
is exactly the same as what I did in my nineteen years' work in
industry.

This book is, in part, the result of my mistakes. I hope that other
people may profit from them.

Acknowledgement

I would like to thank Cambridge Communication Limited for allowing me access to any material which was produced during my nineteen years with the company.

1 In the Beginning . . .

The development of the means of communication

A long long time ago, perhaps more than a million and a half years ago, a creature picked up a stone with one hand. He was able to do this because he could put his thumb right across the palm of his hand. Then he picked up another stone with his other hand. He was able to do this because he could stand on two legs. Then he banged the two stones together. They shattered. He looked at the pieces, chose the one with a sharp edge, and shambled off. He was a man: *Homo*. In other words: this animal had upright posture, opposable thumbs, and a brain big enough and developed enough for him both to assess the usefulness of sharp stones and to make them.

Because it was a very long time ago he is sometimes called 'early man' and, because he actually looked more like a chimpanzee than you and me, 'ape man'.

Tape your thumbs to your index fingers, and you will find out for yourself how important that opposable thumb is.

Life went on, maybe for nearly one and a half million years. We know that this early man chipped pieces off lumps of flint, to make them a more usable shape for hammering and to give them an edge for scraping and cutting; these have been found and can be dated approximately. Some of them were quite beautiful. We also know that early man had started to become the lord of creation. His brain, as the size of its case shows, began to grow bigger: very much bigger than that of any other animal. He learned to use the sounds that he could make; one sound meant 'look out', another meant 'meat', another meant 'stone'. He had quite a lot of sounds which meant something to other creatures like him. Then one day, as he went out of the cave where he lived he said, 'I am going to hunt in a different place today.' The woman in the cave said, 'Don't be late for supper, dear.' He had become a clever man: *Homo sapiens*. In other words he was a creature with upright posture, opposable thumbs . . . and language. His brain had become developed enough for him to communicate complicated messages to his fellow creatures. He looked quite like you and me.

We are told by physical anthropologists that *Homo sapiens* was, and is, an 'undifferentiated animal'. In other words he has no special characteristics for defence, attack or escape which help him to survive. He has no great size, like the elephant; strength, like the lion; speed, like the deer. His teeth are small, his claws are weak and brittle. They are no use as weapons. He has no horns. He can neither see nor hear particularly well, and his sense of smell is poor, so he can easily be taken by surprise. Yet he has outclassed all other animals. This must be because his big brain, his upright posture, his tool-making ability made that possible. But, above everything else, his developed brain enabled him to speak. Speech is man's most important attribute, as it enables him to communicate with other men.

It is obvious that birds and most other animals communicate with each other, and some after a fashion with man. It is equally obvious that this kind of communication is very limited. Animals and birds can give warnings of danger to each other. Your cat or dog can communicate to you that it wants to go out, or come in, or be fed; and a dog will let you know that there is a stranger around. Cats and dogs can communicate pleasure, displeasure and pain. They can let you know that they don't like Mrs Brown, but they can't tell you that it is her hat that they don't like about her. You can tell them that you are going out, that you are sorry to leave them, and that you will come back as quickly as possible, but it is unlikely that this will be understood. Members of the parrot family 'talk', but this is simply imitation of sounds, not proper speech. Even man's closest relations, the chimpanzees, cannot be taught to speak in a meaningful way. Speech makes possible the communication of a great deal of information that is both specific and complicated.

Speech is the ability to make sounds which have meanings to other people who can make the same sounds which have the same meanings. Speech then becomes language, which is a learnt and not an inborn faculty, and belongs to a specific group of people. Language makes communication both easy and, at the same time, difficult. The connection between sounds and meanings is largely arbitrary, unless it is onomatopoeic like *bang* and *pop* and *splash*, and languages can be very different from one another. Having a common language implies that information can be shared and passed on from one person to any other who is near enough to hear what is being said. Communication in any detail is impossible if people do not share the same language. It is easy enough in a shop to indicate that you would like to buy a tube of toothpaste if it is visible; comparatively easy to mime if it is not – except that you may be presented with a toothbrush instead of the paste. It is much more difficult to ask, without language, if it is likely to rain tomorrow; and virtually impossible to ask for someone's views on, say, predestination. Even if a language *is* shared, distance beyond earshot makes communication by speaking impossible. This problem man has tried to overcome in various ways.

The Bantu-speaking tribes of southern Africa use two very simple methods. The first, shouting, depends partly on the language, which has few vowels and those it does have possess great carrying power; partly on the technique employed; and partly on the terrain. The shouting takes place from one hilltop to another, in climatic conditions which give the maximum amplification. The second, whistling, does not depend, as might be expected, on imitating set phrases, since long and unusual messages can be transmitted. Curiously enough, there is a whistling language in Gomera in the Canary Islands which is still in use, although the telephone is rapidly supplanting it. The 'talking' drums of West Africa have become notorious, but in fact they are used simply to send news and instructions and abusive messages between nearby villages. By the use of two or three drums, the tones and rhythms and general shapes of sentences can be reproduced. The Indians of North America used smoke-signals for sending messages over greater distances than their voices could carry.

Distance may be said to have two dimensions: space and time. If messages could be sent by various means to combat distance in space, there still remained the problem of time. When the message had been sent and received, there was nothing left, except in the minds of the sender and receiver. There is little doubt that for thousands of years man needed no permanent communications. After all, he possessed very little. Obviously we know nothing of ownership at the time, but in a Stone-Age hunting and gathering society a subsistence economy was all that was possible. It can only have been a day-to-day existence. There was no need for records or recording.

When agriculture and animal husbandry came into being, so too did the notion of ownership and property. The keeping of records became necessary if only as notches in a stick or knots in a leather thong to show numbers.

Such primitive societies still exist, and they have no written language. Some members of these societies have prodigious memories, particularly for relationships among members in the community. It doesn't particularly matter, of course, if a great-great-grandfather's name is remembered incorrectly. The number of cows owned by an individual or a family will certainly be remembered correctly, and a tally will be kept.

The first great advance in combating distance in communication also solved the problem of permanence: the invention of writing, some five thousand years ago. Picture-writing preceded writing proper; but the difficulty of representing anything but names by pictures led to the development of ideographs (symbols denoting abstract concepts); however, ideographic writing requires an immense number of symbols. Alphabetic writing, in which each symbol represents a speech sound, developed around the eastern shore of the Mediterranean about 2000 B.C. As *writing* involves using symbols for language, the translation of these symbols back into language is *reading*. Writing and reading are therefore complementary activities.

The two great early civilizations where writing developed were Sumer in the Tigris–Euphrates valley and Egypt in the valley of the Nile. Here people had come to live in concentrated groups. Cities grew up with temples and palaces, as well as houses, and there was great wealth. Society had become complex and could only have developed, and been organized and administered, given a written language. Sumerian writing consisted of a system of wedges, made by pressing the end of a reed stylus into a clay table which was then sun-dried or fired. Hundreds of these clay tablets have survived. Mostly they are concerned with trade, the delivery of goods supplied: milk, cattle, wheat, barley, sheep and fish. Business had begun. Clay tablets, although virtually indestructible, are hardly portable. In Egypt, early writing was mostly carved on stone or painted on the walls of tombs. But, by around the year 3000 B.C., a kind of paper, made by beating the pith of the papyrus plant, was coming into use. This was the first 'paper', from which all subsequent paper has taken its name. Chipping stone or gouging marks in clay and baking the result was time-consuming, and so was writing by hand.

The invention of writing and reading as a means of communication also had another drawback: it could take place only between people who shared these skills – and they were usually members of a particular social class or section of the community. (In Britain, clergymen and other members of religious orders and of the aristocracy were virtually the only ones who could read and write – until the time of the Industrial Revolution, when a new upper class came into being. It is interesting to note that the proper name for a clergyman is a 'clerk in holy orders' and that a clerk is a 'worker who keeps files or records'. Illiteracy, both in modern industrial society and in developing countries, is still a communication difficulty.)

For five thousand years writing had to be a one-off process, until typographical printing was invented. It has been claimed that this was the single technological advance which facilitated every other technical advance that followed it. Its impact was tremendous, but we still do not precisely know its origin. Certainly printing preceded typography: the Romans used wooden blocks for making patterns on plaster and textiles, and the Chinese used block-printing for designs and pictures.

The invention of printing as we know it is usually attributed to Gutenberg and took place at the end of the fifteenth century. Even after the 500 years since then, printed language is still the most common method of communication. Laborious typesetting by hand has been superseded first by mechanical, then by electric, then by electronic means. Today we are surrounded by and inundated with printed matter: books, magazines, newspapers, brochures, circulars, forms and posters, a great deal of which is destined to end up in the wastepaper basket. It has been claimed for some years now that the age of paper is coming to an end and that communication will be carried on by electronic means, but it hasn't happened yet.

Writing and printing have advantages over speech: speech is ephemeral, writing and printing are lasting; speech can be misheard, writing and printing cannot. That they can be misunderstood is a separate problem which will be examined later. However, writing and printing need to be conveyed from the sender to the receiver, and this takes time. Just as distance beyond earshot made communication by speech impossible, so distance made communication by writing or printing slow. Quicker ways of sending and receiving information became necessary as the world opened up because of the growth of trade and commerce resulting from the Industrial Revolution in the eighteenth century. Telegraphy, the transmission of written or printed messages by electrical signals, was developed in 1873, although the idea had been mooted as early as 1753. Samuel Morse invented the code which bears his name for sending these messages. By 1862 the world's telegraph system covered approximately 150,000 miles.

The next development in overcoming the problem of distance between people communicating with each other side-stepped printing; this was the invention of the electrical transmission of speech. The name of Alexander Graham Bell is usually associated with the telephone, which he patented in 1876. Soon after, Rutherford and Marconi were experimenting with wireless transmissions, and in 1901 Marconi sent a wireless signal across the Atlantic. Distance was no longer an obstacle to communicating by voice.

We have already made the point that speech is ephemeral. Recorded speech is not. Experiments in recording sound began in the middle of the nineteenth century; Thomas Alva Edison wrote in his diary (18 July 1877): 'There's no doubt that I shall be able to store up and reproduce automatically at any future time the human voice perfectly.' He was right – at least he would have been if he had left out the one word 'perfectly'. Nowadays a recorder of some sort is part of almost every child's equipment in so-called 'advanced' societies, and certainly few households are without one.

Although written or printed words do have advantages over spoken ones, the reverse is also true, as spoken language contains more than words. If the speaker can be seen, facial expressions and gestures can add meaning to the words. Even if he cannot be seen, intonation and emphasis can do the same. The famous speech at the beginning of Charlie Chaplin's film *The Great Dictator* contains no real words but communicates a very great deal. In another famous film, *Night Train to Munich*, the man who says, 'This is a fine country to live in', cheats the Gestapo by changing the intonation of 'fine'.

So far we have concerned ourselves with language as the medium for communication, spoken, written, coded, telegraphed, telephoned, broadcast and recorded. To describe in words a person, a building, a scene or an event is extremely difficult, usually inadequate, and does not make recognition possible. An accurate picture or a photograph or a model makes recognition easy. Not everyone can draw or make models, and doing so takes time, even for those who have the necessary skill. The police are well aware of this, and use identikits, assembled from verbal descriptions, to enable their officers and the public to recognize wanted persons.

The advent of photography was momentous. Although the scientific principles on which it is based had been known for over a century before, it was not until 1839 that the daguerreotype became generally available, and photography proper is less than a hundred years old. First there were black and white photographs; then moving pictures; then coloured photographs and films; then television, first black and white and later coloured; then video recording. Today, cameras, ciné cameras and video cameras are part of everyday life. Pictures alone, however, even moving ones, can rarely communicate adequately. Many thousands of years ago, men painted pictures and made models; we have seen the results of their handiwork in prehistoric caves. What they represent is obvious, but we can only speculate as to their meaning and purpose. The old-fashioned, silent films needed captions, even though the acting in them was mostly mime; foreign films need dubbing; a television programme with the sound turned off is less comprehensible than a silent film, because the acting assumes the presence of sound. It seems, then, that to communicate adequately in all situations, both language and pictures are necessary.

How can we be so sure that *Homo sapiens* has always had a language? It has already been pointed out that man is an unspecialized animal. In the beginning he could only survive in what must have been a hostile environment by making tools and weapons, and by co-operation. He had to hunt for food, and protect himself against the elements and other animals. He had to protect the children of the group and care for them in their long maturation period. He had either to care for the old and infirm or dispose of them.

No group of people has ever been discovered, however primitive, in which each person did what he liked, when he liked, with whom he liked. For a collection of people to live together – even if only a family group like that of the Kalahari bushmen – there must be structure, organization and rules of conduct. These have to be transmitted from person to person and from generation to generation. Language is essential but, with no written language, knowledge cannot be accumulated beyond what can be held in the memory and so little progress can be made. Technology can improve but only very very slowly. Archaeologists estimate that some one and a half million years passed from the time when man first discovered that he could make tools and weapons by chipping pieces of flint to the time when he began to use metal. Civilization was impossible.

It is no coincidence that writing was invented in the Tigris–Euphrates valley and in Egypt, where people had begun to live in concentrated groups, to own property and to trade.

Today, we have a tremendous range of means of communication which has taken tens of thousands of years to develop. The advent of *Homo sapiens* has been dubiously dated as around 50,000 years ago. Most certainly he had language, so about 45,000 years passed before language was written; an additional 4,000 years passed before language was printed; only 500 more before it could be transmitted over distances beyond man's hearing, and less than 100 before our so-called advanced technology of communication was developed. Inventions are often made in different places and at different times. What we call progress is not universal and lineal; today, while part of the world has an almost unbelievably 'high' technology, there remain primitive and peasant communities, little different from those of what archaeologists call the Stone Age.

This book is concerned with communication in business. A great deal of this originates in a company's office: letters, notices, minutes, memos, forms, brochures, manuals. These may first be written by hand, or dictated to a shorthand writer or into a recorder. (Shorthand, popularly supposed to have been invented by Pitman in England and by Gregg in the USA, is actually of great antiquity. There was a system of Latin shorthand in the first century B.C.). After being dictated, the communication is usually typed. The typewriter was invented slightly before the telephone, and was produced commercially by Remington & Sons, USA arms manufacturers, in 1874. Superseding typewriters, which have passed through the manual, electric and electronic stages, are word processors, which are computerized typewriters.

In the last quarter of the nineteenth century, an up-to-date office would have contained a telephone and a typewriter for sending out its communications. Today, there will usually be, in addition to these essentials, a copying machine; a telex which transmits typed messages all over the world; a visual display unit to display information obtained from a computer; and a television set adapted to receive teletext information. All this hardware can do no better than reproduce what is put into it. As the computer people say: 'Garbage in, garbage out!'

The purpose of this book is to help people who, by the nature of their jobs, are likely to be busy to put less garbage in.

2 Why Bother?

The importance of communication in business

We have taken a look backwards at the 50,000 or so years which have elapsed from the time man developed language to his producing the high technology of communication we possess today. Why, after all this time, is there concern about communication in general, and business communication in particular?

There is nothing new in bothering about getting the correct message across, if it is thought to matter. Before literacy was general, the churches did their best to communicate the stories and beliefs of Christianity with painting and sculpture and the dramatization of the Bible stories and the liturgy. The churches have recently shown a new awareness of the need to close the communication gap. The New English Bible, the vernacular Mass in the Church of Rome, and the Alternative Service Book in the Church of England bear witness to this. Many, particularly those who have been brought up to know them well, prefer the Authorized Version of the Bible, the 1662 Prayer Book and the Latin Mass, but these all pose problems of communication for the majority of people.

Now, government, the Civil Service and, above all, industry and commerce have joined in, and at least pay lip-service to the need for clear communication. That such a need exists, and is ever growing, can be demonstrated.

As we have seen, in the beginning man could only have survived if he could co-operate intelligently with his fellows in order to overcome the dangers of the environment. For this intelligent co-operation he needed language. It is perhaps worth nothing that ants and bees, so often held up to us as examples, do not co-operate intelligently. Their difference of function is instinctive and unadaptable. To accumulate knowledge, to organize and run a complex society, man needed writing, which is still the basis of communication today.

For a very long time, writing and reading were the complementary skills of an élite; and power, both religious and secular, was in the hands of that élite. In England, which was mainly an agricultural country, the élite consisted of the aristocracy, other landed gentry, and the Church. People moved about very little, and families lived in the same place for generations. The only transport was provided by horses. News travelled very slowly and mainly by word of mouth. Only the élite needed to be able to read and write.

The Industrial Revolution which began in the middle of the eighteenth century changed all this. England became the first and greatest manufacturing country in the world. Factories were built; towns and cities expanded; steam became the chief source of power, and coal was needed to produce this; canals were dug and railways built to provide transport for the coal, raw materials and manufactured goods. People, as well as goods, moved around. Export trade developed, and ships were needed. The whole fabric of life became more complex. A new élite emerged, that of trade, richer and with a far greater need for communication than the old élite. Vast economic enterprises could not be managed without an equally vast system of communication.

None the less, comparatively few people were involved in this. The majority of the population worked long hours in poor conditions for little money, and were totally at the mercy of their employers. They were, in the main, illiterate.

However, the employers were not all self-interested, and the employees were not all downtrodden, spineless or stupid. Four interrelated organizations came into being: the trade unions, the Co-operative movement, adult education, and the Labour Party. Perhaps most importantly came compulsory and free education.

Robert Owen, a manufacturer, was at the same time a philanthropist; he wanted employees to have more control over their conditions of work. He was instrumental in forming the first trade union, the Grand National Consolidated, in 1834. This collapsed, but in 1851 came the first successful trade union, the Amalgamated Society of Engineers. In 1868 the Trades Union Congress met for the first time, and in 1871 it was granted legal status. Throughout the 1890s the trade union movement supported the formation of the Labour Representation Committee which came about in 1900 and which became the Labour Party in 1906. For the first time the workers had representation in Parliament.

We are not concerned here with the politics of the trade unions and the Labour Party. Our interest lies in the effect they had on communication in industry. Previously the workers had little or no say in their conditions and wages. Communication, such as it was, was one-way, from the employers to the employed. This was not necessarily bad – there were caring and generous employers, as was Robert Owen – but exploitation was the order of the day, and the time had come for change. Communication had to become two-way.

Membership of a trade union and a political party also implied a knowledge and acceptance of the rules, the obligations and the privileges. Communication between organizations and their members was necessary. Previously, membership of the Church, the only institution to which most people belonged, had meant knowing the catechism and the creed which had been learnt by heart, with varying degrees of understanding.

Side by side with the development of the trade unions and the Labour Party came organized adult education. The London Mechanics' Institute started as early as 1823, and the London Working Men's College in 1854. In 1873 the University of Cambridge formed its Board of Extra-Mural Studies, and in 1903 the Workers' Educational Association came into being. Robert Owen started the Co-operative movement which, as well as manufacturing, buying and selling goods and distributing the profits to the members, ran educational programmes, particularly for women. The Women's Co-op Guild aimed to change the subordinate position of women in society, and was to some extent and in some areas successful.

It was obviously a corollary of the emergence of a self-conscious working class that it should be able to communicate. Certainly reading and writing were the minimum skills necessary.

In 1870 came compulsory primary education. Before this, religious bodies had run their own schools, but their concern was rather with spiritual than with economic and social life.

Prosperity was not for everyone, nor for ever. Before the Industrial Revolution, when people stayed in the same locality for generations, the most important units were the family, which was a much wider group than the nuclear family of today, and the neighbourhood. Members of the family and their neighbours would look after the old, the sick and the unfortunate. In the midst of the affluence of the new industrialism was grinding poverty, distress and loneliness. In efforts to combat this, the Friendly Societies grew up. These were voluntary mutual-aid associations, democratically run, with members paying regular contributions to a central fund which provided financial help in times of hardship. Accurate records of these funds needed to be kept, and members had to know their liabilities and entitlements. Like the trade unions and the Labour Party, such societies needed rules which had to be communicated to their members.

Largely through the efforts of Lloyd George, the state came to accept some responsibility for the old and the unemployed. In 1903, old age pensions were introduced, and in 1911 sickness and unemployment benefits. Again, accurate records were necessary. Birth certificates became important. Benefits had to be claimed. The era of form-filling had begun. Bureaucracy was on the way.

Two World Wars, with economic depressions and unemployment following in their wake, made Lloyd George's prophecy of the advent of what Archbishop Temple called a 'Welfare State' come true. In the Beveridge Report of 1942, plans for a comprehensive insurance scheme appeared which became law in the National Insurance Act of 1946. Also in 1946 came the National Health Service Act. These, along with social security (state financial aid to alleviate poverty), theoretically ensured that we are all looked after from conception to cremation. Such a complex, interrelated and overlapping scheme produces communication problems of immense proportions. Masses of information have to be asked for, given, processed and acted on. Thousands of forms are produced by the state alone.

This is not all. When the author was a child, her house contained, apart from furniture and coal fires, gas lighting and cooking, the following items of machinery: a mincer, a sewing machine and a piano, and outside, in the shed, was a bicycle. Compare this with the amount of equipment in even a modest house today, all of which has to be installed, operated, maintained and repaired. Consider the motor car: we buy, lease or hire-purchase it; we tax and insure it; we get a driving licence; we join a motoring organization; we claim from our insurance company. All these things involve communication. And forms.

Similar developments have taken place in business. National Insurance contributions must be collected from employees. Company pension schemes can replace or add to the state scheme. There is massive legislation to protect employees: stringent rules about health and safety at work; rigid conditions for dismissal and redundancy; Industrial Tribunals through which employees can appeal against dismissal. (Curiously enough, there is nothing to stop an employee leaving an employer, however unjust and inconvenient this may be.) Again, a great deal of difficult legal information has to be communicated from the law-makers to those who have to work within its parameters, and to get it wrong can be disastrous.

The story of technical innovation is even more spectacular in business than in the home. The modern office has been mentioned already; the modern factory would be unrecognizable to those living in the time of the Industrial Revolution. Machine breakers of the nineteenth century would perhaps encourage computer breakers of the twentieth. A whole new industry has grown around the computer and, since the first practical machines were built during the Second World War, the development of the application of computers has set the scene for a revolution.

A great computer mystique has grown up which is an enormous barrier to communication. To a considerable number of lay people – and to a regrettable number of business people – the computer is magic; it has a life and will of its own; it cannot be controlled, and is the cause of a great deal of evil, particularly unemployment. That a computer is only an electronic device for performing calculations at high speed, and that it can do only what it is told, is difficult to understand. Perhaps the mystique is enhanced because there are computer languages (Cobol, Fortran and Algol being the most widely used, and Basic for microcomputers) which give the impression that the computer speaks of its own volition. Computer languages are only devices to convert the information fed into it to the binary form in which computers calculate. A binary system is one which uses only two digits, 0 and 1, corresponding to the on/off position of a switch; numbers are expressed in powers of two instead of powers of ten as in the decimal system we are accustomed to. Because of the mystique, which in part is due to the incredible speed of computer calculation, it is difficult to think straight about it. Without computers it would have beem impossible to put men on the moon – and that fact alone makes the belief that they are magic understandable.

From the standpoint of communication, it must be accepted that computers are here to stay; that they only do what they are told, and are able to use only the information which they are given; and that they save an immense amount of time. If the information which is processed is wrong, the result will be wrong. Again, because of the mystique, computers have been used as scapegoats: 'the computer got it wrong' has been given as an excuse for an astronomically inaccurate bill or as an explanation for an incorrect pay-slip and wages which are less than they should be . . . Garbage in = garbage out.

It is interesting that children today accept computers without trepidation, learn to operate them and then to program them in the primary school; for them there will be no mystique.

It may well seem that, in the office and the factory, technology becomes more and more – and people less and less – important. Computers and robots and workers seem much of a muchness. For a long time now there has been an awareness of this, and there has been a deal of talk about job involvement and enrichment, and about participation. There is no doubt that many jobs are deadly boring, and that most industrial unrest comes from those areas where the work is unrewarding. It is also true that members of the Confederation of British Industry, the Industrial Society and other interested and caring people are given to making pronouncements along the lines that most industrial trouble results from a breakdown in communication. Is there a relationship between boring and repetitive work, poor communication, and stoppages and strikes?

It is cynical perhaps to suggest that this must be the case because so many large companies have appointed communications managers or directors and have set up communications departments. The author took part in a large-scale investigation of communication in the UK locations of a multinational company. Some of the comments of the employees are worth recording:

'I shall take a bad view of it if, after our telling management for years, they pay consultants to tell them what we tell the consultants.'

'Everyone talks about company communications and how important they are, but nobody can tell you what company communications they're talking about.'

'Back up communications with fact and positive action, not phoney motivation.'

'I don't have much trouble because if I want information, I usually know who to get it from.'

'They'll ask you to a meeting any time you like but if you ask for a meeting you almost get hung out of the window.'

'We've even had a load of goods arriving from the port without anyone telling us and we've had to phone up to find out what to do with it.'

'Well, she arrived in one Monday morning and her machine had gone.'

The last two statements indicate that even operational information was lacking, and employees who cannot do their jobs properly, through lack of information, are likely to be sceptical about communication in general, which the other comments show. 'If the company doesn't care about us, why should we care about the company' is inevitably an attitude which results; and grievances were made much of and a chance to upset the company gladly taken. The sad thing was that the company did care, and care very deeply, about its employees. It set up a working party, the report of which contained these statements:

The Company should undertake an education process to promote greater understanding of the information provided.

The Board should accept the principle that all employees should have the opportunity to influence decisions which materially affect them.

Lack of communication had resulted in the employees being unaware of their part in the organization; of their importance as 'stakeholders'; of the interrelationship of all parts of the company; of the benefits they received from the company; of the company's position in the total economy; of the financial state of the company and the need to make profits.

Luckily, both for the company and for its employees, it was wise enough to set up a system for the provision of information to serve the following purposes:

> to enable individuals or groups to perform efficiently

> to improve the understanding of the company operations

> to meet the need for general company information

> to enable employees actively and constructively to contribute to decisions directly affecting them

> to meet current statutory requirements on disclosure of information

> to assist employees at all levels to develop a sense of belonging to the enterprise as a whole.

A very large engineering company ran an audio-visual and discussion course for its opinion-makers on what it called the 'economic facts of life'. At the end, a militant shop steward was heard to say to one of the directors, 'Well at least now I know that we're all in it together.'

Communication difficulties in industry are probably proportional to size. In small organizations, where everyone knows everyone else and everyone knows what everyone else is doing, and usually why, the problems are not so great. In large companies, particularly those which operate in different locations, a great effort is required to get through to employees. It is probable that personal contact between senior management and employees is valuable in companies of all sizes, because it makes people feel that someone cares about them.

There seem to be three channels of information in large companies. The first is the orthodox management channel, from senior to junior management who pass the information on to the shop floor.

The second is from management to shop stewards. This double channel is often the cause of friction, as there is the feeling that the shop
stewards know earlier, and more, than junior management. The third
channel is the grapevine. Often the information is conflicting.

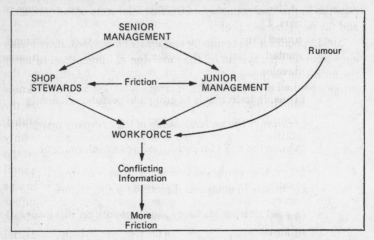

One company's senior management denied strenuously that it was
buying a new factory in a certain place, which rumour had said it
was. Office staff were typing letters about the new factory; telephon-
ists were getting calls to the place; chauffeurs were driving senior
people there; a workforce was being taken on. No doubt management
had a valid reason for not confirming the rumour, but no reason
whatever for denying it, and this caused a great deal of aggravation.
'Do they think we're fools?' was the general cry at the time. No
communication at all is better than giving false information.

The grapevine is worth noticing. It indicates what people have
found out, as in the example above, or what they think they have found
out. If this is wrong, then it should be denied. If it is right, it should be
ignored if, for some reason, it cannot be confirmed. Credibility is of
paramount importance if a company seriously wishes to have good
relations with its employees. It also often shows what they fear: are
they going to be moved? is their factory to be shut down? If they cannot
be reassured, then the hard truth is usually better than lies.

There are certainly some employees who only care about how
much is in their pay packet – but it may be argued that, except in a

minority of cases, this is the fault of the company. What employees want to know is what concerns them, and this is everything to do with the prosperity or otherwise of the company, and of course anything which affects them personally, such as possible redundancy, relocation, a change in the pension scheme, a takeover, a change of working hours. They want to know not only what, but why.

They also need things to be explained in a way they can understand. A factory wanted to increase its production by a third. An impasse situation developed which lasted many months because the employees had asked for a wage increase which management knew was too great. The increase asked for was a third of the basic wage; the logic of the shop floor said that if they increased production by a third, they were entitled to that proportion of increase in pay. It was only when this rationalization was pointed out to management that the problem was finally solved. The management took the trouble to spell out why the calculation wasn't as simple as that, and its pay offer was eventually accepted. (This story may seem incredible, but the author can vouch for its truth, as she was the one who pointed out the logic of the asked-for increase.) This was a clear example of an industrial dispute which resulted from a failure in communication.

It is often assumed that communication in industry is one-way, downwards. This should certainly not be so. Communication upwards can consist of matters other than complaints, although this is not often so; questions and suggestions can go upward by the same path as complaints. There is often a complaints procedure agreed between a company and the appropriate trade unions; this procedure should be communicated to all employees, and everyone should be held responsible for seeing that it is followed. Brushing aside complaints, questions and suggestions is, to say the least, ill-mannered, nor is it calculated to keep a good relationship between management and other employees.

At the time of writing, increasing concern has been expressed at the poverty of employee information given by some major companies which have been accused of paying only the barest of lip-service to the 1982 Employment Act. It is suggested that, unless this is remedied, there may be a need for further legislation. Low morale, absenteeism, high labour turnover, go-slows and strikes must be symptoms of a lack of understanding between management and employees. Perhaps more important still is a lack of common purpose. Why should people give of their best if they don't know what they are giving it for? Failures in communication can cost large sums of money in lack of co-operation. Changing line layout in a factory is an example of a situation which might cause trouble; this would certainly be the case if the shop-floor workers could see no adequate reason for the change.

One very significant change has taken place in education over the last half-century. In the primary schools children are now encouraged to take nothing for granted, but to inquire into reasons. '. . . because I say so' is no longer accepted as an answer either from parents or teachers to the question 'Why?' This change has continued from the primary to the secondary school, and on to further education. Teachers, tutors and lecturers are no longer regarded as omniscient and powerful. What they do and say and teach comes under scrutiny. Equally importantly, students of all ages expect to be consulted about the way in which their school or college is run, and about what course of study they should follow. It is hardly to be wondered at that, when they go out to work, they should expect to have a large say in their company's affairs – particularly where they themselves are concerned.

Relations both inside and outside a company are complex, and all involve communication. Managers talk to managers; employees talk to employees; management talks to employees; employees talk to management; the company talks to trade unions; trade unions talk to the company; the company talks to shareholders, to customers and to the general public.

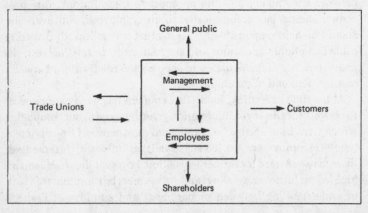

Before any aspects of business communication can be considered, it is necessary to give attention to the basic ingredients of communication: words.

3 Words

Language as the basis of communication

Most people think that they can communicate, and they are upset if told, or it is proved, that they can't, or that sometimes they do not. More often than not they blame the person to whom they are attempting to communicate. They blame him or her for being stupid or not listening, or not reading carefully enough. Being able to speak or write a language, even correctly, does not mean that the ability to communicate is automatically present. We accept that training and practice are necessary to turn an innate ability into a skill in which most people can achieve a reasonable performance and a few outshine the rest. This is not doubted for such skills as running or jumping or acting or singing or painting. Few people get on to their high horse if told they can't run very fast or sing well enough to join the Bach choir, but most do object if told they can't communicate.

There are two communication skills in which it is acknowledged that some people are star performers. Oratory is one of these. Lloyd George, Adolf Hitler and Winston Churchill in their different ways were outstanding examples. Creative writing is the second of these skills, but communication is limited to those who are able and willing to read. Most of us know that we can't equal Churchill or Hardy, but what about the 'reasonable performance'?

The golden rule, we are told, is: 'Say what you mean.' This is not as easy as it sounds. It is particularly difficult when, as is so often the case (as we shall discover), we don't know what we mean. It is even more difficult if we don't realize that we don't know what we mean.

Let us examine this notice which was observed hanging over the lifts in a multi-storeyed hotel:

> ## Please walk up one floor or down two for improved lift service.

Exercise: Before you read any further, please write down (a) what you think is the meaning of this, and (b) how you would have worded the notice. Check with the solution given later.

'Improved lift service': can you improve a lift service? How? Make the lift travel faster? Make it carry more passengers? Not by going up one floor or down two. So, it would be a reasonable assumption that a better lift stops on those floors. The prospective passengers go to find out. They discover that there is no other lift, but there's an identical notice.

We can only assume that the hotel was not offering an 'improved lift service'. The originator of that notice was not saying what he meant. Why should people walk up one floor or down two? On the basis that, generally speaking, it is easier to walk downstairs than upstairs, he wants people to walk if their journey is only a short one. Why? Presumably it is because the lift will then be free for those who want to make longer journeys. So what he meant was: 'Don't use the lift for short journeys.'

Did you get it right? The original notice would have been better if 'for improved lift service' had simply been left out. It is worth pointing out now, and we shall return to this point later, that there is no word in that notice which cannot be understood by any English-speaking visitor to the hotel. They are, all twelve, perfectly ordinary everyday words; but they do not communicate. (It is probably worth adding that the statement on the notice is true: if everyone making short journeys walked, only people making long journeys would

use the lift, and so the service would be 'improved' for those fewer
people.) We must conclude that a perfectly true statement in ordinary words can still fail to communicate.

An electrical tool, seen in a factory, had two labels tied on its
handle. One, put on by the suppliers, read:

WARNING

The batteries in the AH/MSQ-55
could be a lethal source of
electrical power under certain
conditions.

Thinking, no doubt, that the words were equivalent to calling a
spade a digging implement, some wag had added *his* label which
read:

LOOK OUT

This can KILL you

– which has a refreshing directness.

Exercise: Write down why neither of the labels contains an effective
communication. The answer is given in the next para-
graph.

Were the writers saying what they meant? Yes: they were telling
you that the tool can be lethal or, if you prefer it put this way, can

kill you. So, assuming that you need to use the tool, what choices do you have? If you are sensible, you will leave it alone until you discover in what circumstances it can kill you, so that you can avoid these at all costs. In the case of the two labels, neither writer has asked himself what he wants the result of his communication to be, which is that the potential user will use the tool safely. In order to do this, one must know how.

It seems then that, as well as saying what you mean, you must know what you intend the *result* of your communication to be. The writers of both labels forgot that in order not to kill oneself using the tool, one must know how to use it safely. An effective label would have told the user what to do and what not to do, in order to be safe.

As well as too little, some writers of labels and notices cannot resist giving too much information. A tin of custard powder, after giving the instructions for making a pint of custard, adds: 'To make half a pint use half the quantities'; the instructions on a mop head read: 'The plastic backing plate is made in one piece, but is designed to break into two halves when first used. This does not affect the performance of the mop.' It is not advisable to assume that one's readers or potential users are moronic. On the other hand it is advisable, particularly when writing for an unknown readership, to assume a lack of knowledge. It is a difficult feat for one who knows to think himself into a state of not knowing. This problem will be referred to again, particularly in Chapter 12 on user instructions.

Recently there has been a laudable campaign for plain English. That this is only part of the problem of effective communication has been indicated. 'Walk up one floor or down two' is plain enough; so is 'for improved lift service'. But put the two together and non-communication results. 'Look out: this can kill you' is starkly plain, but it doesn't tell you what to look out for.

The two main butts of the advocates of plain English are jargon and gobbledegook. In the new edition of Fowler's *Modern English Usage*, these are considered to be the same thing, although a wish is expressed that the meaning of 'jargon' should be restricted to something like that given in the *Collins English Dictionary*: 'specialized language concerned with a particular subject, culture or profession'.

It is essential to point out that the use of jargon is no bar to communication between people who understand it. To the anthropologist the sentence, 'Cross-cousin marriage is important in a matri-lineal society', is a simple statement of fact. It will probably take the reader, if he is not an anthropologist, some seconds to work out what it means, and he may not succeed then. 'Cross-cousin' and 'matrilineal' are jargon words.

The following sentence comes from a book on structured systems analysis: 'This input–output analysis identifies all the flows of data we can find in the narrative, except for on-demand queries.' It illus-trates one of the pitfalls of jargon: the use of words which have both an ordinary meaning and also a specialized (and different) meaning within a particular subject. Most people know what 'input', 'output', 'analysis', 'flows', 'data', 'narrative', 'on-demand' and 'queries' mean when used ordinarily, but not many laymen will understand the sentence quoted. 'Unconscious' means one thing to the ordinary person and an entirely different thing to the psychiatrist. 'Patho-logical', the dictionary tells us, means 'relating to, involving, or caused by disease'; in computer language it means 'a severe form of coupling between modules where one module refers to something inside another module'.

In the accounts of a large company, under the usual '£ 000' head-ing, is

Extraordinary item   14 900

To the auditors and accountants, 'extraordinary' has a particular meaning. To non-financial readers, the extraordinary thing is that almost £15 million are not accounted for in a more precise way.

Jargon changes as sciences change. The following was found on a school notice-board commenting on the new socio-educational jargon:

I used to think I was POOR
Then they told me I wasn't poor
I was NEEDY
Then they told me it was
Self-defeating to think of myself as needy
I was DEPRIVED
Then they told me deprived
Was a bad image
I was UNDERPRIVILEGED
Then they told me underprivileged

Was overused, I was DISADVANTAGED
I still don't have a penny
I still need COMPENSATING
But I have a GREAT vocabulary.

The breakdown happens when jargon is used to communicate to lay people. It is simply the situation of two people without a common language trying to talk to each other.

Unfortunately there is a certain element of one-upmanship attached to possessing specialized knowledge and its associated jargon. This seems particularly true of those who work with computers and other electronic devices. It would be a great help if people would stop pretending, because they are afraid of being considered lesser mortals, that they understand something when they don't. If there is no reason why you *should* know about programming a computer or installing a washing machine, why pretend that you do? Equally, you should insist that anyone whose job is to explain something to you does so adequately.

Gobbledegook is different from jargon in the author's opinion, despite what Fowler says. The *Collins English Dictionary* defines it as 'pretentious language, esp. as characterized by obscure phraseology'. It is now a common pastime, especially on television shows and in newspapers, to find and expose examples of gobbledegook. It seems that some of the chief perpetrators are those who purport to explain pension schemes.

Exercise: Here is one example, which you can try to unravel before you read any further.

> 'Final pensionable wage' is the average of the member's pensionable wage on the three 6th days of April preceding the normal retirement date, or the date of retirement or death whichever is the earlier.

Presumably the member of the scheme trying to work out his pension entitlement needs to know his 'final pensionable wage'. As this booklet is obviously for non-salaried employees, it is unlikely that he will be accustomed to this kind of language. To begin with, the notion of 'three 6th days of April' is bewildering. There is usually one '6th day' of any month. Then there is the suggestion that the member has retired at the normal time, also earlier, and died as well. As the calculation is the same for these three situations, there is no need to list them. There is no mention of late retirement, so perhaps it doesn't exist. So what does the member need to know, and to do? He needs to know, and add together, his wage on the last 6th April he worked or will work, and that of the year before and the year before that, and divide the answer by three.

Those who write gobbledegook like this will be happy with other similar writers, as the jargon writers are with one another.

Exercise: Before going on, try to unravel this, which defeats the author. (She has put her suggestion later in the chapter.)

> For the purposes of this part of the schedule a person over pensionable age, not being an insured person, shall be treated as an employed person if he would be an insured person were he under pensionable age and would be an employed person were he an insured person.

Lawyers are also great gobbledegookers, and they combine this habit with a lavish use of jargon. They add another feature: saying the same thing three times. We leave our possessions to our 'heirs, successors and assigns'; we have 'covenants, conditions and agreements'; we 'have, hold and possess'. It seems that lawyers write for other lawyers, foreseeing possible disputes, rather than for their clients. The author asked for a simple will to be drawn up, leaving her possessions equally between her son and daughter. The result was a 'last will and testament' consisting of several pages of, to her, largely incomprehensible legal language – and anyway, what is the significance of 'and testament' to the ordinary person?

The people who write jargon usually speak it as well, while gobbledegook seems to be only a written language. It is difficult to imagine a pensions manager saying those words about 'final pensionable wage'. He would be much more likely to say what we have decided was necessary to tell the scheme member.

As well as jargon and gobbledegook, there are 'in', 'vogue' and 'buzz' words. These become, as the names suggest, fashionable for a short time and do little, if anything, to help communication. At the time of writing, 'basically' is one of these, and it usually means something like 'the first thing I've thought of in answer to your question'. These words are better avoided altogether in business communication. Does 'in this day and age' mean more than 'now'?

Clichés, Fowler tells us, are stereotypes. They are phrases which have become so common as often to have lost their meaning, and can be facetious, as 'to sleep the sleep of the just'! Let politicians explore avenues and leave no stones unturned, but let business people simply find out.

It is claimed by some that meaning is obscured by long words and long sentences. The Fog Index is one measure of the readability of written language. This is a system worked out by Robert Gunning and explained in his book *The Technique of Clear Writing*. He described writing which is difficult to take in as 'foggy', hence the name. To calculate the Fog Index, a passage of a hundred words must be chosen. The average number of words in each sentence is found by dividing the number of complete sentences into the number of words in those sentences. The / number of words with three or more syllables is next counted. Words beginning with a capital letter, those ending with -es or -ed and compound words like 'lawn-mower' are left out. The average number of words in the sentences is added to the number of words of three or more syllables, and the result multiplied by 0.4.

Exercise: The last paragraph, up to the oblique line, comprises 100 words. Calculate its Fog Index (FI). The answer is to be found below.

This is what the FI is supposed to indicate:
a score of under 10: the passage can be easily read
scores of 11, 12 or 13: bright children can read it
and scores of 14 and upwards: only those with a higher education can do so.

Working out the FI of the marked passage a couple of paragraphs ago:

there are 6 complete sentences

there are 99 words in those sentences

the average number of words per whole sentence is
$99 \div 6 = 16.5$

the number of words with three or more syllables is 5

$16.5 + 5 = 21.5$

$21.5 \times 0.4 = 8.6$

the FI of the passage above is 8.6

Before agreeing that this is a useful way of checking business communications, these two criteria (long sentences and polysyllabic words) should be considered. Long sentences usually mean that there are several clauses and unnecessary words. The following sentence comes from an employees' handbook:

> Where, however, the additional day (or days) is attached to the annual holiday period which, in itself, already includes one of the eight National holidays, qualifying conditions for payment will be maintained in accordance with paragraph 8(b), viz., there will be one qualifying day for payment, namely, the working day following the holiday.

Long sentences, yes, we can probably agree that they are undesirable; but are words of three or more syllables really difficult to read and understand? There are many words of three syllables in ordinary business use, and some of four and five; for example 'committee', 'quotation' and 'commercial' have three; 'mechanical', 'conservative' and 'continental' have four; 'administration', 'organization' and 'accumulative' have five. So the use of the FI should be carefully considered. It must be remembered at the same time, however, that it has been established that those newspapers and magazines with the highest circulations have an FI of under 10.

People who write sentences like the one just quoted are really gobbledegookers. There is also a pomposity which is apparent in the answer to a civil servant who wrote to ask if he could be given a certain book which he needed for his work. The letter said that he couldn't, but that he was 'authorized to acquire the work in question by purchase through the ordinary trade channels'. The letter writer, had he spoken the reply, would no doubt have said: 'No, but you can buy it.'

There are accepted differences between spoken and written English. Most people have three languages: The first is that which is spoken every day in ordinary circumstances, at home, at work, in the pub. The second is that which is spoken in special circumstances, talking to the boss or the vicar, giving a lecture, or being interviewed. Then there is a written language which, except for very personal letters, is different from both the ordinary and the special, although it comes closer to the special.

Spoken language of either sort can be subdivided again: when the speaker can be seen and when he cannot. Even when he can be seen, there are two possibilities: (a) when, as well as being seen, he can be interrupted and replied to, as in ordinary face-to-face conversation; and (b) when he can only be seen and heard, as in a film or television programme. The usual situations that apply when the speaker cannot be seen are when he is talking on the telephone or radio, or when he has made a recording.

The main difference between everyday and special language lies in the degree of precision and the use of slang. 'The old man wants you on the blower' becomes 'The Managing Director would like to speak to you on the telephone'; 'The telly's on the blink' turns into 'There's an intermittent fault on the television set'; 'The quack's given me some jollop' would be translated into 'The doctor has prescribed some medicine for me'. These two languages do merge into each other. Between 'The old man wants you on the blower' and 'The Managing Director would like to speak to you on the telephone' comes something like 'The MD wants you on the phone'. In fact, a relationship exists between the manner of speaking and the degree of familiarity between the people concerned.

In the spoken language of anyone, the speaker does not need to rely on words alone. If he can be seen, both facial expression and gesture can add to the meaning. In some cases, facial expression can qualify words. 'You are a nuisance' said with a straight face means one thing, but, said with a happy smile, something different. Gesture can add emphasis: a clenched fist making the movement of banging on the table, although not actually doing so, shows that the speaker feels strongly about something. If he cannot be seen, the speaker's intonation and emphasis are particularly important, as the examples in the first chapter show.

When speaking in a face-to-face situation, there is less need to structure what you have to say or to be quite so precise. Feedback is immediate, and questions can be asked and disagreements expressed. This is not so in broadcast talks or recorded messages, or in church sermons (which the author has always thought to be a pity).

When speaking other than in a face-to-face situation, the content of what is said must be planned and structured. Points should follow each other in a logical fashion. As questions cannot be asked, there should be no need for them. Nothing, however, can be done about disagreements.

Spoken English is not as formal as written communication, and speakers are usually forgiven for small grammatical errors, such as split infinitives. Fashions change; whereas once it was considered incorrect to follow a singular noun by a plural verb this is now accepted, and is certainly heard on BBC programmes. The 'government' consists of a lot of people although it is only one entity, and so is often followed by 'are' instead of 'is'.

The question of regional accents is a hotly debated one. In business, the accent used in spoken communication must be 'acceptable'. What makes an accent 'acceptable' is difficult to define. It may be something to do with whether people from outside the speaker's area can understand what is being said. However, some *unacceptable* accents are as easy to understand as *acceptable* ones; but they are not equally liked, certainly in boardrooms, so we may suggest that understanding is not the only factor which determines acceptability.

Written English, certainly in business communications, should be correct, brief and straightforward. It is an interesting phenomenon, however, that there are many ordinary people who can communicate adequately, or even well, when they are talking but, the moment they pick up a pen or sit down in front of a typewriter, they seem to feel a need to use words, phrases and constructions quite different from those of their normal speech. Their ability to communicate to all intents and purposes disappears. There follows a list of words which appear in writing with their spoken equivalents. You are invited to add to the list, as you come across additional examples:

Written	Spoken	Written	Spoken
ensure	make sure	edifice	building
commence	begin, start	transpire	come about
assemble	put together	assist	help
inscribe	write	endeavour	try
residence	house / flat / bungalow	proceed	go
inhabit	live in	purchase	buy
conflagration	fire	sufficient	enough
inform	tell	attired	dressed
acquaint	make known	inquire	ask
accommodation	housing / home	provided with	given
ablution	wash	ascertain	find out
ameliorate	improve		

The people whose minds become blank when faced with a piece of paper to write upon, as well as the gobbledegookers, should try to say what it is they mean, probably into a tape-recorder, before they attempt to write. If they get tongue-tied when attempting to record, the safest thing is to sit down and say what they mean to another person, and then to write it down with the other person's help. They should, of course, choose someone who will tell them when they are talking rubbish.

Business communications are not intended to be great literature, but a clear and pleasant style should be aimed at. Consideration must be given to finding the correct message: 'Don't use the lift for short journeys' instead of walking up or down stairs. The depth of knowledge (if any) of the receiver of the message must also be taken into account. There is no need to explain beta-blocking to a doctor, but the doctor usually needs to explain this to a cardiac patient. As was said earlier, we can't all be great communicators, but we can achieve an acceptable standard if we try hard enough.

The author's tentative suggestion for the meaning of the pension gobbledegook (page 40) is:

> a person who has retired [presumably from employment where he was *ipso facto* insured] will be treated as though he is still working, i.e. paying his insurance – or, rather, having it deducted from his wage or salary.

It has been shown that language is not the only barrier to communication, although the anti-jargon and anti-gobbledegook people give the impression that it is. Much more important are the thought processes which take place, or should take place, before a communication of any significance is made.

Exercise: Below is an extract from the handbook which accompanies a portable electric typewriter:

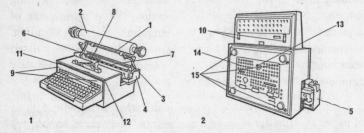

REMOVAL OF COVERS

The side covers are retained by the attachment springs on either side of the machine, which may be accessed by lifting the paper bail (1-1). The platen (1-2) is held by the retaining levers (1-3) which must be raised to extract the platen. The cover (1-4) and the paper table assembly (1-7) are removed by loosening the cover screws (2-5) and disconnecting them from the attachment clips (1-8). Before this can be done, it is necessary to remove the paper trough (1-6). The keyboard cover, secured by two hexagonal bolts (1-9) and captive clips (2-10) is removed to allow the keyboard to be cleared. The typebar cover (1-11) held in situ by hinge springs and screws (1-12) is then lifted off. Turning a captive screw (2-13) loosens the inspection cover (2-14) and removing the four base plate screws (2-15) allows the chassis to be cleared, thus completing the dismantling procedure.

Sort out what has gone wrong with the thinking of the writer who produced these instructions. The answer will be found in Chapter 12.

We have already discovered that saying what you mean is not easy, and that it involves two other considerations: (1) to whom are you communicating, and (2) what you want the result of your communication to be.

Let us eavesdrop on a pharmaceutical company's salesman visiting a doctor to tell him about one of the company's drugs. Communicating to a doctor means that he can use medical terms without having to explain them. His message must be as brief as possible, taking into account the information he has to get across, as doctors are busy people. He must be sure of his facts, or he will be discountenanced. He wants the result of his interview to be that the doctor will prescribe *his* company's drug, therefore he must point out its virtues and explain why it is better than rival companies' products. He must use only facts to persuade.

Communicating to a known homogeneous group, like doctors, is probably easier than, say, writing a booklet to explain a share option scheme to all the employees of a company. To explain something quite complicated to a group of people with a wide range of knowledge and abilities means that, without being condescending, the language must be jargon- and gobbledegook-free, no specialized knowledge may be assumed, and the explanation must be absolutely clear and never ambiguous.

In this book we are not concerning ourselves with advertising, which uses words and phrases with emotive overtones. Very rarely in business communication do we need to persuade by the use of emotional phraseology. How powerful it can be is illustrated by taking this short extract from one of Churchill's best-remembered wartime speeches:

> You ask, 'What is our policy?' I will say: 'It is to wage war, by sea, land and air, with all our might and with all the strength that God can give us; to wage war against a monstrous tyranny . . .

and turning it into plain English: 'In answer to your question about our policy, I have to tell you that it is to wage total war against Nazi Germany.'

4 Who Are We Talking To?

Networks of communication

If we want to come to terms with proper communication in business, we must accept that using plain words, and avoiding jargon and gobbledegook, will not necessarily result in getting the correct message across. Most important is our awareness of what the result of the communication should be. So we must know who talks to whom in industry and why.

To start at the top, 'Industry' itself is communicated to by the government through Acts of Parliament. There is no escape from this legislation which controls so much of business activity, from setting prices to restoring any disturbance in the environment which the company may have caused. Those who have to operate within its parameters must be completely aware of what is involved. Ignorance is not accepted as an extenuating circumstance if you break the law. Most of this legislation is difficult to take in and apply to your own circumstances. Many companies, especially those without qualified accountants, fail to understand the Value Added Tax regulations correctly; the penalty for getting them wrong is heavy. Also heavily penalized are infringements of the Health and Safety regulations, however hard the employer may have tried to enforce the correct safety standards but failed. As an employer you have to bear in mind the Sex Discrimination and Race Relations Acts when appointing new staff and fixing wages and salaries. Probably most irksome to employers are the regulations about dismissal, and the subsequent Industrial Tribunal you will have to attend if you fall foul of them. Someone has to be responsible for keeping within the law. In a large company it will be the Personnel Director or Manager. In a small company it may be the Managing Director who has to add this to all his other duties.

Reading the Acts as they appear on the Statute Books is not helpful. Because of this, and because people need help in interpreting the law, there is a thriving industry in the 'Plain Man's Guide' type of books; these must be checked carefully before you can feel safe to rely on them, or disaster may result. Algorithms or 'pathways through the legal maze' are to be recommended. These are discussed in Chapter 11.

The Confederation of British Industry serves as a communication link between the government and industry. It is itself a strong advocate of effective communication; from time to time the CBI issues warnings about the folly of industry in not paying enough attention to employee communication, and of the government in not paying enough attention to industry's needs.

There is also communication between various industries and their appropriate trade unions. This can be conducted on a national level, as between British Rail and the National Union of Railwaymen, and between British Coal and the National Union of Mineworkers. (It is worth considering whether, had communication between the latter two bodies been better, the miners' strike of 1983–4 would have continued as long as it did.)

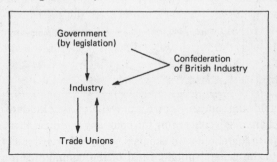

Each individual company has a large network of communications. Very important is that between management and the employees, and this will be considered in detail later in this book. All those things which an employee should know, or must know, in order to do his job satisfactorily, have to be communicated to him in some way. It may be only Bill telling Joe when it occurs to him, or perhaps something brings Joe's lack of knowledge to Bill's attention. The employee must know the terms and conditions of his appointment; this is usually communicated by letter, and is codified in a contract of employment. He will want to know details of his obligations and benefits, and these will often be set out in an employees' handbook. Some things, such as a pension scheme, a share option or profit-sharing scheme, will be explained in detail in special booklets, or possibly in audio-visual programmes. If he is lucky, the newcomer will have some kind of induction training, so that he gets to know something about the company for which he is now working. He will get news of what is going on from the company's monthly broad-sheet. He may be instructed in the various policies and procedures of the company. He will look for day-to-day communications on the notice-board. He may have the company's job-evaluation and appraisal scheme explained to him. He will receive some training for his job. All this, and a lot more, comprises the company's communication to him.

He will also receive communications from his shop steward, who will tell him what his rights are as an employee of the company, and what are his obligations to his trade union. He will be instructed in any grievance procedure which has been agreed between the company and the trade union.

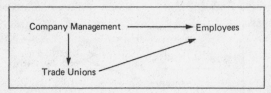

Outside the company's own four walls, various kinds of communication are made concerning the company to different sectors of the public: to shareholders, customers, prospective customers or clients, and to the general public. Most of the communication to shareholders is made by the Stock Exchange in the national press, quoting the current share prices. There is a statutory obligation on all companies to produce an annual report and accounts, and to hold an annual general meeting which all shareholders have a right to attend, and where they can vote on any issue. Anything of interest which happens to the company is reported in the press, which the general public as well as shareholders can read.

The annual report and accounts contains the obligatory financial information which is prepared by accountants and certified as correct by them. There is no obligation to present this information in any but the conventional accountancy way. A considerable number of shareholders in public companies are people who are totally ignorant of accountancy and to whom a phrase like 'movement of fixed assets' is utterly confusing, because if assets are fixed they can't be moved. The financial information is usually accompanied by a lengthy and euphoric report of the company's activities over the year just ended, with splendid coloured photographs of, say, the new sports pavilion, the Chairman talking with royalty, and various other matters which contribute nothing to an understanding of the report. If shareholders who do not understand the accounts would only complain, a comprehensible report for the non-financial ones among them might be included. Some companies enclose a copy of the employees' report along with the shareholders' report. These glossy reports are extremely expensive to have produced and printed.

By 'customers' is meant those people who actually buy the company's products, be they typewriters, toasters, pills and potions, computers or aeroplanes. The most badly treated in terms of poor communication are those who buy ordinary office or domestic equipment and find the accompanying instruction books useless. Chapter 12, on user manuals, examines this subject. However, it is not only small business equipment which suffers in this way. One example, given in that chapter, concerns the makers of a very large continuous furnace, who provided no adequate instructions as to what to do should an emergency situation develop.

Communication to prospective customers comes through the various media. There are advertising agencies and public relations companies which specialize in this, and the subject is beyond the scope of this book. Advertisements on commercial television channels are apparently very successful, which means that they must bring enough new sales to justify their enormous cost. To the ordinary communicator, the irrelevance of most of these advertisements is bewildering, so the rules governing other types of communication obviously do not apply here.

Communication to the general public obviously also comes via the media. In fact, any member of the general public is a potential customer, a potential shareholder, and a potential employee; general press, radio, and television coverage is therefore important. A company which is always featuring in the news because of its strikes and lock-outs will not attract new employees or shareholders; a boss whose name appears regularly in the press because he is involved in industrial tribunals is unlikely to get many applications for jobs.

Sometimes, when something of interest is happening to a company, not only can it get free publicity, it can also to a certain extent control the contents of a story, by issuing a press release; however, this control is limited, because press releases are often cut, and the cutting can destroy or distort the message. A press release should, if possible, be structured to make cutting easy. This may be helpful for whoever does the cutting, but it is particularly useful in ensuring that the story goes out right, if briefer than was originally intended. When issuing a press release, always give a name and telephone number so that a particularly interested newspaper editor can easily get additional information. Newspaper editors are perfectly aware of the 'free publicity' angle of press releases, and unless the story is really 'news' it will not be published.

Company brochures, like shareholders' reports, tend to be a lot of gloss and little message. This may be because they are often multi-purpose. A brochure aimed at encouraging graduates to apply for jobs is unlikely to attract clients, customers or investors. It is worth considering producing separate brochures for separate purposes, prepared by experts.

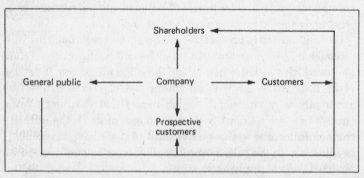

All a company's communications, put together, add up to the total image of that company; its stationery, letters, telephone manners and messages, training materials, booklets, audio-visual programmes, advertisements, newspaper articles, shareholders' reports, press articles. All of these should be given proper attention; otherwise the image will suffer.

For even a small company, it is a worthwhile exercise to have a communications 'stock-taking'. This should preferably be carried out by specialists in communication who will examine all the information put out to and from any source, except that which is the speciality of advertising agencies and public relations companies. In assessing employee information, a distinction should be drawn between operational and other information. Operational information consists of the instructions necessary to enable employees to carry out their jobs satisfactorily, and will therefore include training. Ideally, an outside examination should be made of both kinds of information, but it is better that they are not confused. Included in such a stock-taking would be talks with employees at all levels in the company, to get their views on existing communications and on possible methods of improvement.

The result of the stock-taking would be an objective assessment of the existing communication set-up, and recommendations for improvement, if this is thought to be necessary.

Communication is an art and a science. A belief still exists that anyone can do it, but this is not true. However, this does not mean that only the expert need bother about getting a message across; it means that everyone can achieve that 'acceptable standard' which was referred to in Chapter 3; but some people are, or can be, very good communicators. It should be one of these people's special responsibility in any company, large or small, to make sure that all communication is as effective as it can be. That does not mean that the person on whom the responsibility falls must do it all alone. We would expect television commercials to be made by experts; why then should the employees' handbook be produced by someone in the personnel department lacking the special expertise communication demands? The pensions manager may know all about pension schemes, but he certainly does not know all about communication. Above all, beware of the expert trying to communicate his expertise; often he cannot see the difficulties which can beset the ordinary person.

The general principles of communication having been examined, the time has now come to consider detailed applications of these principles in the business situation at the present time.

5 As Others See Us

The image of the company revealed in its communications

The image of a company is derived from many sources: from its impressive buildings, glossy brochures, fantastic TV commercials, large and small advertisements in the national press. However, for most people the first real contact with a company comes by way of a letter or telephone call and sometimes the image is then tarnished. For a smaller company, often our first awareness of its existence comes in the same way, and so a good or bad impression is created.

Paperwork

Letters are an extremely important part of a company's total communications. There are three aspects to a letter: the paper on which it is written, the way the content of the letter is laid out, and the message it contains. All three are worthy of attention.

A certain amount of information must, by law, be shown on the writing paper of a limited liability company: the name of the company, the registered number and place of registration; and the address of the registered office. Clearly, the address from which the letter is sent (which is often different from that of the registered office), the telephone and telex number should also be included. All that information, unless it is very carefully arranged, could take up half of the usual (A4) size of a company's writing paper. Some companies have half-size paper for very short letters, which makes the problem worse.

Both the printed part of the writing paper and the paper itself must look pleasant and be in good taste. Good taste is to some extent a matter of opinion, but it would not be appropriate for a city firm of accountants to use flimsy pink writing paper with the information printed in ornate script. The paper on which the information is printed should be of a reasonable quality, but not so thick that it can hardly be folded to go into an envelope.

The 'letterhead' of business stationery consists of the name, address, telephone and telex numbers of the company; all the other statutory information is generally printed in small type at the bottom of the page (the 'tail'). If the company has a logo, this is usually put at the head, and as logos are often decorative, this can add to the good appearance of the writing paper. It is worth having the letterhead (and tail) properly designed by professionals rather than knocked up by the typist or the man in the drawing office whose usual job is producing plans for building sites.

However well designed the paper is, it can easily be spoilt by the letter typed on it. There are certain conventions in the layout of letters which change from time to time. Nowadays, the date and the name and address of the person to whom the letter will be sent are typed on the left-hand side of the paper, and without punctuation. This, one assumes, is in the interest of speed, and as it does not detract from meaning, there is no objection to it. Oddly enough, it is considered incorrect to write the date in its shortest form (i.e. 4.6.88), and the name of the month should be spelt out in full, although 'st', 'nd', 'rd' and 'th' following the day can be omitted. A reference may be inserted over the date, and this will be repeated in the answer so that the letter can be easily identified.

If you are writing to an organization rather than to a particular person, the letter should begin 'Dear Sirs'. If you are writing to an individual, the letter should begin 'Dear Sir', 'Dear Mr Jones' or 'Dear Henry', depending on how well you know the person to whom you're writing – but if the style is 'Dear Henry', this should be hand-written, not typed. Each paragraph should begin at the left-hand margin, and not be indented. If you begin 'Dear Sir', you must end 'Yours faithfully', otherwise 'Yours sincerely'. Under your hand-written signature, your name and title or position in the firm should be typed. If there is one, 'enclosure' should also be typed under the signature. It tells the recipient of the letter to look for the enclosure, and it reminds the typist to put it in. The body of the letter should be punctuated to make sense.

If a letter is to reach the person for whom it is intended, it must be addressed correctly. Conventions change, as has been said; whereas 'J. Brown, Esq.' was once considered correct for a man, now 'Mr J. Brown' is acceptable. How to address a letter to a member of the titled aristocracy or to a Church dignitary is set out in various publications. The difficulty comes with ladies. If all you know is that you are writing to Mary Brown, is she Miss, Mrs, Dr, Lady or what? This is one reason why, under the signature in a letter, the title and name should be typed. There is a way round the 'Miss or Mrs' dilemma, and that is to use 'Ms', pronounced 'Mizz', a word that is hardly ever spoken except when dictating a letter!

The letter should be spaced to look well in the size of the paper available, neither so squashed in at the top that there is a great white space underneath, nor so close to the bottom that there is not enough room for the signature to be properly written.

If more than one page is necessary, subsequent sheets should be of matching plain paper. At the bottom right-hand corner of the first page, either 'continued' or '/', followed by the last word of the page should be typed. On the second and any subsequent pages, the page number should be typed at the top in the middle of the line. The recipient's name should be typed on the left-hand side with the date on the right-hand side, in case the pages get mislaid. To make doubly sure, the name of the company can also be typed. Either 'continued' is typed at the bottom of the page and is repeated on the left-hand side of the new page, or '/' followed by the last word on the page, is typed at the bottom and that word is repeated with the oblique stroke after it on the fresh page. See the two examples on page 58.

Clarity and brevity are the keynotes of all communications, including letters. People in business are busy, and they do not want to read more than is necessary. Flowery assertions that 'our customers' interests are always our first consideration' and 'assuring you of our best attention' are a waste of time in dictating, in being typed and in being read.

Printed writing paper is not the only stationery which a company uses and which is sent to people outside. Compliments slips often serve instead of a short letter. To attach one of these to a brochure is quicker than writing a letter saying that you have much pleasure in sending the requested literature.

```
         ...  be augmented by on-the-job training.   This can


                                          continued ...
```

```
                            -2-


A. Bloggs, Esq.
Acme Engineering Company Limited                    26th June 1986

... continued
frequently be costly when judged upon unit results ...
```

```
         ...  be augmented by on-the-job training.   This can


                                                    /can
```

```
                            -2-


A Bloggs, Esq.
Acme Engineering Company Limited                    26th June 1986

can/


frequently be costly when judged upon unit results ...
```

Exercise: List all the faults in the letter on page 59. A list of the faults
appears at the end of this chapter.

THE ACME ENGINEERING

COMPANY LIMITED

SWAVESEY

CAMBRIDGE

Tel. Swavesey 54321

19.6.86

Dear Sir,

    Thank you for your very kind enquiry which we had much pleasure in receiving. We shall be glad to supply you with the machine spares you require at the current list price which is shown in the parts list enclosed. Please complete the order form which is also enclosed, and send it with your remittance to the above address. We will then forward the spares you have ordered at our earliest convenience.

    We assure you of our best attention at all times, and remain

Yours Sincerely

J Smith

J. Smith

Visiting cards are extremely important, and the same rules apply to their design as to writing paper; they should state the name of the card-holder, his or her position in the company, the name of the company, its address, telephone and telex numbers. As with writing paper, the logo is often included. A neat, uncluttered card gives the best impression. There is no standard size for business cards, but it should not be more than 9.5 × 5 cm to fit into the usual containers – and as the purpose of a card is that it should be kept for reference, it is more likely to defeat this purpose if the card is an awkward size.

An invoice must have printed on it the company's name and its registered VAT number. On it must appear: the date (to establish the tax point); what the invoice is for; the cost; and the VAT at the appropriate rate. If the invoice is sent to a company it should be addressed to the company and not to an individual. 'For the attention of Mr D. Jones' can be added, to expedite payment. An example is shown on page 60.

Employees in a small company usually communicate with each other verbally, either face to face or using the internal telephone

THE ACME ENGINEERING COMPANY LIMITED

SWAVESEY
CAMBRIDGE
CB4 5QJ

Telephone Swavesey 54321

March Motors Ltd
Industrial Estate
MIDDLETON   Suffolk
SK2 1BL
For the attention of J. K. Brown Esq.

Order number 427

Invoice number 427
Invoice date   July 2
and Tax Point   1986

Quantity	Description	Unit price	Net price
6	Widget clips	£2.80	£16.80
6	Widget washers	£1.40	£8.40

	Total	£25.20
	Plus VAT @ 15%	£3.78
	Net amount due	£28.98

Terms   Net 30 days

VAT no. 247 3345 61

system. Even in a small company there are occasions when the person you need to tell or ask something is absent. Under these circumstances, you can scribble a note on an odd piece of paper – but this stands a good chance of being overlooked or swept to one side – or you can use a properly designed form which will help remind you to give the right information: from whom, to whom, and date or time of writing. If you are passing on information received by telephone, it could be very important to know at exactly what time that call was received. In large companies, when people are separated by several floors or corridors and the internal phone isn't answered immediately, memorandum pads can be extremely useful, provided there is some standard procedure for distributing the memos, and this should not be too difficult to devise.

The telephone

Apart from letters, the other main contact with the outside world is made by telephone. There are, of course, two sides to this: calls coming in, and calls going out. For both of these the voice, speech and manner of the telephonist or receptionist are of the utmost importance. The telephone distorts the voice slightly, and some sounds can be difficult to distinguish. Care must be taken to speak very clearly, without sounding absurd. British Telecom has a recommended phonetic alphabet:

A = Andrew	H = Harry	O = Oliver	V = Victor
B = Benjamin	I = Isaac	P = Peter	W = William
C = Charlie	J = Jack	Q = Queenie	X = Xmas
D = David	K = King	R = Robert	Y = Yellow
E = Edward	L = Lucy	S = Sugar	Z = Zebra
F = Freddie	M = Mary	T = Tommy	
G = George	N = Nellie	U = Uncle	

When answering the telephone, there must be some greeting, and the name of the company must then be stated clearly, followed by 'Can I help you' – although there is a tendency in the modern office to cut out these niceties. Having discovered the caller's name and company, she must then connect him to the person asked for. In doing this, she must repeat the name and company of the caller to the person being called. It is extremely embarrassing not to know the name of the person you are talking to, and equally so not to know whether you are talking to Mr Robinson of Acme Engineering or Mr Robinson of the VAT office.

Major problems can arise when the person wanted is someone of importance. Then the caller must be connected to the secretary of that person and it is her job to take over from there. Busy people must be protected from calls which are time-wasting, and each company should develop its own technique for doing this. Saying that someone is out when he obviously isn't will only get the company a reputation for rudeness; saying that Mr Smithers is engaged at the moment, but Mr Johnson can almost certainly help, is one way of dealing with this problem. Incoming calls should always be answered immediately; it is discourteous to keep people waiting in any circumstances.

If the person the caller wishes to speak to is not available, and a message is left, it must be carefully written down, read back to the caller to check its accuracy, and put on the desk of the person concerned.

Printed telephone message pads are useful, as they make sure that the necessary information is obtained: the date and time of the call; the caller's name, company and telephone number; the person to whom the call was made; the message; the name of the person who has taken the call. This last piece of information is important since when the message is received, if there is any query, the right person can be asked.

An answer-phone is a business necessity, as it is not always possible for calls to be made in a company's working hours. A request on the answer-phone for any kind of response should be meticulously followed up.

Calls going out are expensive in terms of money and time; they should be carefully organized to waste neither money nor time by being made in the cheaper period if there is no reason for not doing this. Timing calls is sensible: to make a call just after the company you want to speak to opens for business may be wasteful if the person called usually talks to one or two colleagues before he settles in his office: the caller will have to hang on while a search is made; time is wasted and the cost of the call mounts up. On the other hand, if the person is known to go straight to his office as soon as he arrives, and he is always on time, this might be the best time to reach him.

Calls should not be made until the caller has worked out exactly what information he wishes to give and/or receive. Notes should be made so that nothing is left out. To continue a call saying, 'I'm sure there is something else I wanted to ask you' is unbusinesslike. Notes should also be made during the call. Not to know whether it was 14.30 or 15.30 that was arranged means another call. The diary must be consulted when making an arrangement, otherwise, again, another call will be necessary. A problem can arise when you are efficient and brief, but the person you are talking to rambles on at your expense. One must never sound rude. People who make a lot of telephone calls generally have their own technique for dealing with this: a well-trained secretary, at a known signal, can tell you that Mr Brown is on the other line, thereby cutting short the current phone-call.

One drawback of telephone conversations is that (unless a recording device is used) there is no evidence of what has been said. It is important that the date and time, and the maker of the call should be recorded. A telephone book logging calls is essential in a well-run office. If anything of importance emerges from a phone conversation, a letter confirming this should be sent at once.

Sometimes it is the telephonist, but often it is the receptionist who is the first person a caller has contact with. The same rules apply for her, but not only must the receptionist give a good impression by her voice and manner, she must also look good. She must put callers at their ease, make them feel welcome, and give them any information they need.

The application form

Another area where accurate communication with people outside the organization is essential is when recruiting new staff. A chapter in this book deals with the design of forms; but the communications provided for would-be employees should be so designed that only suitable applicants would be interested, and more than just an application form is required. An advertisement in a newspaper or magazine is the probable first step. Care should be taken in selecting the most suitable journal, and also the best day of the week for the advertisement to appear; this is often very important if a local paper is involved. It is now illegal to specify that a man only or woman only is required, unless there is an adequate reason for doing so. Presumably if the job involves lifting very heavy weights, a company is permitted to ask for a man; and if it involves modelling ladies' fashion wear, a woman.

To save time and postage in sending forms to applicants, the advertisement should give information which will exclude many unsuitable people: 'with a proven sales record' . . . 'shorthand 110 wpm and typing 65 wpm' . . . 'good knowledge of spoken and written French and Spanish' . . . 'clean driving licence and own car essential' . . . 'degree or equivalent qualification in chemistry' are definite things which people either have or have not. 'Good personal appearance' . . . 'able to get on with people' . . . 'pleasant telephone manner' are matters of opinion, and will serve no useful purpose if included in the advertisement. 'Small office' will put off those who like working in a crowd; 'able to travel' will stop mothers with young children from applying; 'irregular hours' will deter people with definite commitments at certain times.

The application form must be designed to find out exactly what it is necessary for you to know. An analysis of the requirements of the job is essential before the form is designed. A health record is necessary: if an applicant had measles or whooping cough twenty years ago, it really does not matter; if he has a heart condition now, it may matter very much. Probably a medical examination is more useful than a section of a form to be filled in. A curriculum vitae supplied by an applicant is apt to be lengthy and largely irrelevant. Printed questions to answer are better, but they must be carefully worded; 'details of education' may produce a list of schools from a day nursery onwards, when secondary school(s) onwards is all that is required.

With the application form should be sent information about the company, and more about the job than could appear in the advertisement. Salary, if there is a definite grading, should be stated; 'to be negotiated' leaves the matter of salary open, and most companies are prepared to pay more, within certain limits, for an outstanding person. Hours of work are important as they can affect domestic arrangements and also may cause difficulties in travelling to and from work if public transport or car-sharing is involved. Pension schemes, allowances and benefits should be clearly stated, but not in detail at this stage. Holiday entitlement can be a deciding factor for some people. If there is a 'no smoking' rule within the company building, attention should be drawn to it at this stage, as there are still smoking addicts with us. If membership of a trade union is compulsory, this should also be made clear. All this information should produce a second 'weeding-out' carried out by the applicants themselves.

When the application forms have been scrutinized, an agreed number of candidates must be selected for interview; these will be the ones whose answers to the questions on the forms suggest that they most nearly fit the job description. They must be sent a letter telling them where the interview will be held, with a map if there is likely to be any difficulty in finding the place; the date and time of the interview; and the name of the interviewer. This last piece of information is often omitted, and the person who signs the letter may not be the one who conducts the interview. The candidate is given confidence if he knows who to ask for when he arrives, rather than having to say, 'I've come for the job.'

The interviewer will have made notes about any point he wishes to discuss on each candidate's application form. He will also have prepared a list of questions to supplement that information, but he should never ask these as though reading from a questionnaire.

Interviewing is a very difficult skill. It is, unfortunately, another one of those aspects of communication that most people think they are very good at. Very few are conscientious enough to keep records of the subsequent performance of those employees they have interviewed and appointed, in order to find out how many mistaken selections they have made. Unfortunately it is impossible to tell how good the rejected candidates would have been.

Most people being interviewed are nervous. This may make them behave in several uncharacteristic ways: they stutter and stammer or keep twisting a handkerchief; some react in the opposite way and look so nonchalant that they seem not to care; or they talk far too much and far too fast. Allowance must be made for this kind of reaction, but how much allowance is a difficult question, since the successful applicant may sometimes have to work in conditions of stress. The good interviewer will make him or her feel as much at ease as possible.

Careful notes must be taken at interviews, as it is all too easy to confuse people, particularly if they are seen one after another. Descriptive notes are helpful: 'red wavy hair, grey suit with green blouse'; 'very neatly turned out'; 'very blue eyes and a nice smile'. It is polite and helpful to tell the candidates when you will let them know the result of the interview.

As well as writing to the unsuccessful applicants to tell them that they have not been selected, a letter of appointment must be sent to the successful candidate. It must say:

>what the job is
>
>when it is to begin
>
>the salary offered and any system of increments
>
>the hours of work
>
>the holiday entitlement
>
>what the pension scheme is
>
>any other benefits, e.g. medical insurance
>
>any requirements: using own car and the allowance made for doing so.

A written acceptance of the job and its conditions is required.

Selecting the wrong person is very expensive in both time and money. It is worth a lot of effort to get it right.

Getting all these things right makes a company look and sound good, and they should receive the attention they deserve.

Solution: The letter on page 59 contains the following mistakes:

Setting out

>The company's address has no post-code
>
>There is no reference
>
>The date is wrongly abbreviated
>
>The name and address of the person to whom the letter is written is left out

'Dear Sir' requires 'Yours faithfully' (neither 'faithfully' nor 'sincerely' should begin with an upper-case letter)

J. Smith has no identification under his signature

The indentations do not follow the modern style of letter writing

'Enclosures' is not typed at the bottom of the letter

Content

The first and last sentences serve no purpose

The letter is wordy and unbusinesslike

A better version:

```
            THE   ACME   ENGINEERING
              COMPANY   LIMITED

                      SWAVESEY
                      CAMBRIDGE
                      CB4 5QJ

                                  Telephone Swavesey 54321


Our reference  JLS/ML
Your reference JKB/BB

19th June 1986


J K Brown Esq
March Motors Ltd
Industrial Estate
MIDDLETON  Suffolk
SK2 1BL

Dear Sir,

Thank you for your letter of 16 June 1986.  We can supply you with the
machine spares you require at the current list price.

A parts list is enclosed and an order form.  If you will complete the
form and return it, the spares you order will be sent within seven
days.

Yours faithfully
```

J Smith

```
J Smith
Manager Spares Division
```

6 Nem. Con.

Communication in meetings and committees

Committee, a portion selected from a more numerous body (or the whole body) to which some special business is committed. *Chambers Twentieth Century Dictionary*

Committee, a group of people chosen or appointed to perform a specified service or function. *Collins English Dictionary*

Meeting, an organized assembly for the transaction of business. *Chambers Twentieth Century Dictionary*

Meeting, an assembly or gathering. *Collins English Dictionary*

Committees must have meetings, in order to carry out whatever is their special business or function. Is there any difference between a committee meeting and a meeting? If we take as an example a voluntary organization, it will have been formed by people with some common purpose or interest and, in order for it to function, it must have a committee, in this case people chosen (usually) by all the members voting. This committee will be given certain powers and, in order to run the organization, must meet regularly.

There may be subcommittees which perform specialized functions, perhaps organizing visits, or writing the newsletter. From time to time, meetings of the whole organization will be held, the most important of which will be the Annual General Meeting.

It would seem, then, that a committee has an executive function and its meetings enable it to carry out this function, whereas a meeting is more general in character. A committee is responsible to a larger body, and must therefore report back to it. Thus it will be seen that a whole network of communication comes into existence.

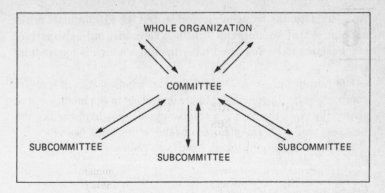

Committee and other meetings can be formal or informal or any stage in between, but in business they are mostly formal.

The structure of a large company is extremely complex, and its most important committee is the Main Board. Next in the hierarchy will be the Board of Directors of divisions, then of companies in the divisions, according to the structure of the company.

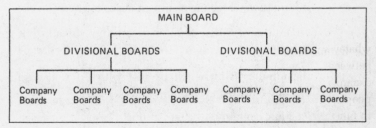

This committee structure produces vast communication networks. In a small company the Board of Directors will be the committee running the business.

Some meetings must be held by law, the most important of these being a company's Annual General Meeting (the AGM). This must be held once every calendar year, and not more than fifteen months must elapse between one AGM and the next. All shareholders must be invited, and given 21 days' notice; the invitation must state that it is the AGM. (Any shareholder who cannot attend may send a proxy who can vote on his behalf.) The law also states that certain matters must be dealt with at the AGM: Directors' and Auditors' reports (which must have been sent to all shareholders), fixing the

Auditors' fees, the fixing of dividends, and the appointment or re-appointment of Auditors and Directors. The notice must also specify any business to be discussed other than that which is required by law.

The purpose of an AGM is the same, whether it is of a major company or a village society: to communicate to the members (the shareholders, in the case of a company) what has happened in the past year, and what the plans are for the forthcoming year.

The communications which have to be prepared are:

before the meeting:

> the notice of the meeting

> the agenda

> any information to supplement the agenda

> a chairman's agenda which contains any additional information which the chairman needs to know

at the meeting:

> the minutes (which will be sent with the notice and agenda of the next meeting)

The notice must contain

> the name of the organization

> the date of the notice

> the place of the meeting

> the date and time of the meeting

> the name of the person calling the meeting

> the type of meeting.

The date of the notice is particularly important when the notice must be received a statutory time before the meeting – 21 days for an AGM – and an allowance must be made for postal delivery time.

If even one member does not receive the notice at the right time, the total business of the meeting may be made invalid.

If the place of the meeting is not well known to all members, the exact address and possibly a map should be included. It is advisable as a check of accuracy to give both the day and date of the meeting, e.g. Wednesday, 8 June, 1988. This helps members to enter the meeting in the correct place in their diaries. If the meeting is an AGM, it is essential to say so.

A typical notice of a formal AGM would be:

THE ACME ENGINEERING
COMPANY LIMITED
SWAVESEY
CAMBRIDGE

Annual General Meeting

Notice is hereby given that the Annual General Meeting of the Company will be held in the Memorial Hall, High Street, Swavesey, on Wednesday, 4 June 1988, at 14.30, to receive the report of the directors and the auditors for the year ended 31 March 1988 and to transact the business on the agenda which is enclosed with this notice.

By order of the Board

P. Robinson, Secretary

Although not always stated in the agenda, most meetings begin with

apologies for absence

minutes of the last meeting

matters arising

and end with

any other business [AOB].

The agenda is a list of the headings of items of business. They will be set out in the order in which they are to be discussed. This order needs careful thought, particularly if one or more items will be controversial and there will probably be a lot of discussion. Important matters should be considered early in the meeting when people are fresh, tempers are not frayed, and no one is watching the clock.

The headings should be ample enough for members to give the subject some thought before the meeting. 'New telephone system' might mean either that the company proposes to install a computerized telephone at a high cost, or that during the lunch-hour the answer-phone will be used. A note after 'New telephone system' such as 'Using answer-phone in the lunch-hour' would lead members to think along the right lines and avoid wasting the time of a member who otherwise would have spent ages finding out all that Telecom can offer.

Writing the minutes of a meeting is a difficult communication exercise. Sometimes they are taken by the official secretary, and sometimes there is a minutes secretary. The minutes should be informative enough for a member who was absent to gather what happened at the meeting and to remind those who were present, without being a verbatim account. The agenda will serve as the framework, but accurate notes must be taken throughout the meeting. The minutes will be signed as a correct record, and names, figures and amounts must be accurately recorded. It is important that a distinction be made between what is essential and what is not – and this is true of all communication.

It is obvious that, whether the meeting is large or small, its business complex or simple, someone must be in control; this person is the chairman. A good chairman not only makes the meeting proceed smoothly, he cuts down very considerably on the time taken. He must be completely familiar with whatever is to be discussed; able to stop irrelevant discussion, without preventing those who have something useful to contribute from doing so; and able to deal with awkward situations. Furthermore, he must be completely impartial. It is a very skilled job, and really efficient chairmen are good communicators.

Any member of a meeting may present a case. This will most likely be in the shape of a formal proposal, or motion, and must be submitted to the secretary in time to be included in the agenda of the meeting. There must be a proposer and a seconder for each motion. The rules for proposing a motion are the same as those for making any presentation, but the procedure can be summarized:

formulate the motion clearly and succinctly

obtain your seconder

accumulate your facts

discard repetitions and irrelevances

put the facts in logical order

send your motion and any supporting material to be circulated with the agenda

consider the objections which will be made to your motion and find the answers to them

canvass your supporters

prepare what you and your seconder will say at the meeting

be ready to accept sensible amendments.

After they have been proposed and seconded, motions may be altered by amendments. Amendments must not negate or completely change the original motion. Like the original motion, they need a proposer and a seconder, and have to be voted on. A motion with one or more accepted amendments becomes a substantive motion which in its turn is voted on, and must be accepted or rejected.

If a member believes that the meeting is not proceeding correctly, he can call the chairman's attention to a 'point of order'. A point of order may be that there is not a quorum present. (A quorum is the number of people who must be present at a meeting in order that it can officially take place. A company's articles of association fixes what this number is.) Other points of order may be that what is being discussed is not on the agenda; or that the speaker is straying from the agenda; or that he is introducing matters outside the terms of reference of the meeting: 'ultra vires'; or that he is using unacceptable language. It is the duty of the chairman to decide on points of order.

The following terms, which have not been defined in the text, are used at meetings:

addendum another word for amendment.

ad hoc Latin for 'for this'. An ad hoc committee is one set up for a special purpose, say to organize a flower show. At the end of this, it ceases to be.

co-opted member someone who is not a regular member of a committee but is asked to join because of some special contribution he can make, like a nurseryman to the committee organizing a flower show.

ex officio Latin for 'by virtue of office'. An ex officio committee member is one who is not elected but is there because of what he is, for example, the accountant on the finance committee.

nem. con. Latin in full *nemine contradicente*, which means that no one is against a motion, but that some have abstained from voting; it is therefore different from 'carried unanimously'.

rider another name for addendum or amendment.

sine die Latin for 'without date'. A meeting which is adjourned without a date being fixed for its resumption is said to be adjourned sine die.

7 Heard It on the Grapevine

Communication inside the company

Induction

When a new employee starts work, he will have already received information when applying for the post, will have been interviewed and told more about the company and what his particular part in it will be, and will have asked for any information that he has thought he needed to know. He will have received a letter of appointment setting out the conditions of the post, and will have written a letter of acceptance.

This last exchange of letters is not a legal contract. Although an employee has no statutory right to an employment contract, the law does require an employer to provide a statement, within 13 weeks of starting work, which sets out the most important points of the relationship. This can be part of the letter of appointment; but usually a contract is drawn up by the company's solicitor, and is therefore written in the customary mixture of gobbledegook and jargon. It must contain:

> a job description (the wording should not be unreasonably vague)
>
> the date when the job started (this is important because certain legal rights are acquired after specified periods of employment)
>
> salary or wages, and any benefits
>
> hours of work, and any regulations about overtime
>
> holiday entitlements
>
> illness and sick pay
>
> requirements for notice of leaving (there are legal restrictions for both employers and employees)
>
> disciplinary and grievance procedures.

Two copies are signed by the contracting parties (the company's representative and the employee), and each keeps a copy.

On arrival, he is usually given a copy of the employees' handbook. This tends to be a very small booklet, presumably designed this way so that it can easily be carried in a pocket which it rarely, if ever, is. This smallness results in the information being squashed up, which makes it look forbidding and difficult to read. One very good handbook, something which is rare to find, was spoilt by being produced in this manner, whereas if it had been A4 size it would have been excellent. Usually a handbook needs updating from time to time, if the employee stays with the company long enough, and a loose-leaf cover makes this easy.

The contents are usually an amplification of the letter of appointment, and a slightly more comprehensible version of the contract of employment. 'Slightly more comprehensible' because the example in Chapter 3, of a sentence which has a lot of clauses and which came from an employees' handbook, is part of the section on holiday entitlement:

Payment for Bank or Other Holidays and Additional Holidays

(7)　　Payment shall be made to every manual worker on the eight National holidays and two additional holidays. The payment shall be computed on a uniform working day of 8 hours for all workers whether employed on dayshift, nightshift, or other methods of working.

(8) (a)　Workpeople shall not qualify for payment for the eight National or other holidays who fail to work the full normal working day immediately preceding and the full working day immediately following the holiday, unless they can produce evidence to the satisfaction of the employer that their absence was due to causes beyond their control.

(b)　Notwithstanding the foregoing, it is agreed that where a paid holiday is included in or attached to the annual summer holiday period, the qualifying condition in respect of the working day preceding the holiday will be waived. The qualifying day in respect of the working day following the holiday period will be retained.

(c)　When one or both of the two *additional* days are attached to National holidays, qualifying conditions as provided for in paragraph 8 (a) will operate and will be applied to all the days of holiday. Otherwise, the two additional days will not carry any qualifying conditions.

(d)　When the additional day (or days) is attached to the annual holiday period, there will be no qualifying conditions for payment. Where, however, the additional day (or days) is attached to the annual holiday period which, in itself, already includes one of the eight National holidays, qualifying conditions for payment will be maintained in accordance with paragraph 8 (b), viz., there will be one qualifying day for payment, namely, the working day following the holiday.

Exercise: What obligations must an employee fulfil in order to be paid for the eight National and two extra holidays? How would you convey this information in an employees' handbook? A suggestion is given at the end of this chapter.

If the company is small, there will be little need to communicate much more information about it than newcomers already know or will soon find out for themselves. On the other hand, when they join Acme Engineering they may be vaguely aware that it is part of a larger company which has a central office somewhere in London, and unaware of the fact that it is part of an immense multinational organization. An audio-visual programme explaining the structure of the company can be very helpful, particularly as it can be seen and heard at any time and, if necessary, by only one person. A well-produced diagram of the structure of the company shows a lot, but not as much as an audio-visual programme. Better still would be the audio-visual programme accompanied by the diagram or a small hand-out. Employees are often interested in a map showing the various locations of the company.

This is one kind of induction programme. Another kind is related to the work which the newcomer will be doing and can be a basic introduction to the training which will be given. Again, as trainees will not all start work at the same time, a self-instruction programme will be most useful. It can be printed, it can be audio-visual, or it can be put on a microcomputer, and it can be planned to make sure that all trainees arrive at the same stage of knowledge or competence before they start proper work.

Some parts of the employees' handbook will need amplification, in particular that part which refers to the pension scheme. Few things in ordinary business life are as difficult for most employees to understand as pension schemes, or are as important to them. It is very hard when aged 26 to think of being 60 or 65, and equally hard to think of dying before retirement and leaving a widow and dependent children. Interest in pension schemes increases proportionately with age. None the less, every employee must belong to the state scheme, or to a company scheme, or both. Some company schemes are contributory and some non-contributory. The language of pension schemes needs to be explained: normal retirement; lower earnings limit; scheduled average weekly pay; pensionable service; commutation; capital transfer value; guaranteed minimum pension; voluntary contributory scheme; maximum lump sum. The best way of explaining a pension scheme is by a specially designed booklet, using diagrams where possible. These will be considered in more detail in the next chapter.

Audio-visual programmes can help in communicating pension schemes, but something is needed for later reference as people forget very quickly, and a booklet is essential. There are a lot of off-the-shelf programmes on various aspects of pension schemes but, as always, some are good and some are not. Employees should know that the company pension scheme is financially independent of the company, which is reassuring in days of economic uncertainty. The role of the Trustees should be explained, since they protect the employees' money. Programmes on those matters which are common to all schemes can just as well be bought ready made, providing that they really communicate, as this is much cheaper than having them specially made. The last people to write explanatory booklets or the scripts for audio-visual programmes about pension schemes are those who know all about them.

Company reports

Since it became obligatory for public companies to disclose financial information, the majority of them have produced versions of the annual report and accounts specially for employees; these soon became known as Beanos or Chick's Owns. Again, they can be good and helpful or they can further confound confusion. They tend to contain pie charts and cakes and bar charts, as it is easier to see proportions than to work them out. A bar with a line a quarter of the way down is easier to take in than what it means if £7,250,000 is being spent out of £29,000,000. Diagrams to help employees understand their company's finances will be considered in the next chapter.

It is also quite usual for an audio-visual programme to be made to explain the annual accounts, usually with the voice of the Chairman,

Managing Director, or Financial Director speaking. Whoever produces these programmes usually assumes too much knowledge of finance on the part of the employees. In one such programme, the employees were told that there had been a profit of £43 million, that £60 million were to be spent on this and that, and that a profit-sharing scheme was to be introduced. The employees must have wondered how they would share minus £17 million!

Profit-sharing and share option schemes can also be difficult to explain. The aim of these schemes is to give employees of a company an added interest in its profitability and to encourage productivity. Profits are sometimes shared by giving employees bonuses, but more usually by making them shareholders. There are usually restrictions on the shareholding, and conditions which have to be met. Share option schemes usually consist of saving for a specified time, and either taking the money saved or using it to buy shares at a specified price. The most common misconception is that an employee is simply given shares which he can immediately sell. Setting out the conditions is a difficult task, and again it should be done by someone unfamiliar with the scheme who extracts the information from the expert. Diagrams are not so helpful in explaining these schemes. The following example shows that the diagram really adds nothing to the explanation.

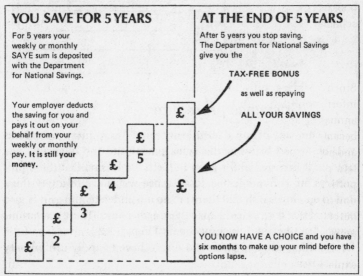

YOU SAVE FOR 5 YEARS

For 5 years your weekly or monthly SAYE sum is deposited with the Department for National Savings.

Your employer deducts the saving for you and pays it out on your behalf from your weekly or monthly pay. It is still your money.

£ 2
£ 3
£ 4
£ 5
£

AT THE END OF 5 YEARS

After 5 years you stop saving. The Department for National Savings give you the

TAX-FREE BONUS

as well as repaying

ALL YOUR SAVINGS

£
£

YOU NOW HAVE A CHOICE and you have **six months** to make up your mind before the options lapse.

Job evaluation

Job-evaluation and appraisal schemes are often a source of industrial conflict, particularly when they are explained badly. An audio-visual programme can be extremely helpful. The main difficulties arise in explaining how job descriptions are written; what benchmark jobs are; how jobs are compared with one another; how the value of each job to the company is assessed; and how the wages or salaries of employees reflect that value. These systems tend to be complex. There are several well-known ones and, of course, they differ from each other. Great skill is required in communicating how they work because, if the employees think the scheme unfair, there will be trouble.

Illustrated below is a frame from a slide-tape presentation and on page 81 is a page from a booklet on job evaluation; both are clear and informative.

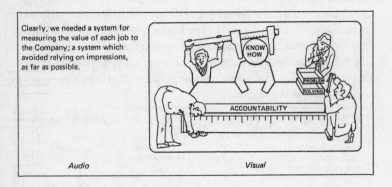

Clearly, we needed a system for measuring the value of each job to the Company; a system which avoided relying on impressions, as far as possible.

KNOW HOW

PROBLEM SOLVING

ACCOUNTABILITY

Audio   *Visual*

Grievance procedures

In a company of any size, grievance and disciplinary procedures will be agreed between the management and the relevant trade unions. It is essential for good industrial relations that these procedures are communicated to all those who have to apply them and to employees, so that there are no misunderstandings. It is also essential that both sides keep to these agreements. There are various ways of setting out these procedures. On page 82 is an extract from an algorithm made to guide those who have to apply disciplinary procedures.

8. DISPUTED JOBS — FACTOR COMPARISON

In preparing the Job Description, the Analyst has set out a number of Job Factors — what kind of thinking the worker must do; what kind of physical work he has to do; what responsibilities he has; and what his working environment is like.

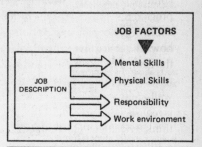

The individual factors of the job are now compared by the Assessment Panel, and the result is a Factor League Table for benchmark jobs.

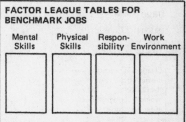

On the basis of these factors, the disputed jobs are compared with the benchmark jobs, and a total factor score for each disputed job is arrived at.

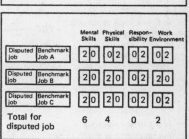

The Panel now has before it —

(a) a job whose grading is in dispute;

(b) a total score for each factor of that job, after comparison with the factors of the benchmark jobs;

(c) a set of Factor League Tables for benchmark jobs.

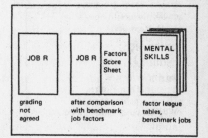

Guide to disciplinary procedures

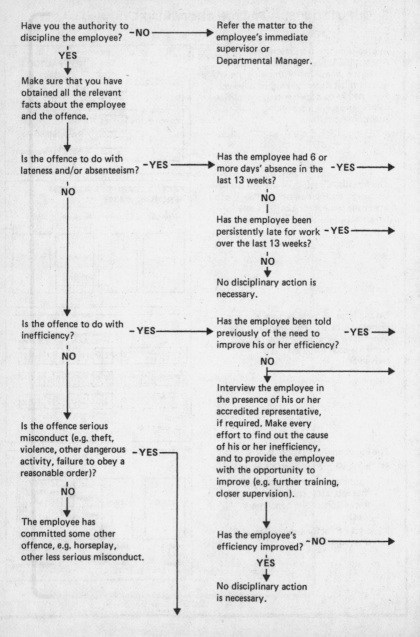

Have you the authority to discipline the employee? —NO——→ Refer the matter to the employee's immediate supervisor or Departmental Manager.

YES

Make sure that you have obtained all the relevant facts about the employee and the offence.

Is the offence to do with lateness and/or absenteeism? —YES——→ Has the employee had 6 or more days' absence in the last 13 weeks? —YES——→

NO

NO

Has the employee been persistently late for work over the last 13 weeks? —YES——→

NO

No disciplinary action is necessary.

Is the offence to do with inefficiency? —YES——→ Has the employee been told previously of the need to improve his or her efficiency? —YES——→

NO

NO

Interview the employee in the presence of his or her accredited representative, if required. Make every effort to find out the cause of his or her inefficiency, and to provide the employee with the opportunity to improve (e.g. further training, closer supervision).

Is the offence serious misconduct (e.g. theft, violence, other dangerous activity, failure to obey a reasonable order)? —YES——

NO

The employee has committed some other offence, e.g. horseplay, other less serious misconduct.

Has the employee's efficiency improved? —NO——→

YES

No disciplinary action is necessary.

This chart sets out quite clearly the complaints procedure:

The new Agreed Procedure

YOUR COMPLAINT IS DISCUSSED WITH

		TIME LIMITS
1	Supervisor/Foreman	1st day
	IF NOT SETTLED	2nd day
2	Departmental Manager	3rd day
	IF NOT SETTLED	4th day
3	Departmental and Divisional Managers	5th day
	IF NOT SETTLED	6th day
	Plant Manager or Labour Relations and Industrial Engineering Manager	7th day
		8th day
4	IF NOT SETTLED	9th day
	Meeting convened by the Factory Personnel Manager at the request of the Convenor of Shop Stewards	10th day
		11th day
		12th day
5		13th day
	IF NOT SETTLED	14th day
		15th day
		16th day
	Meeting of Director of Personnel and the District Official of the Union with appropriate members of both sides	17th day
		18th day
		19th day
		20th day
		21st day
		22nd day
6		23rd day
	IF NOT SETTLED	

7 CONCILIATION and/or ARBITRATION

Company newspapers

There are two kinds of company newspapers: those which appear weekly or monthly, and those which are produced when there is something special to communicate, for example the annual report and accounts, news of a company merger, or a plea to cut down waste. In small companies where a full-size coloured newspaper cannot be afforded, a newsletter may be a substitute.

Whether a newspaper or newsletter is produced, there are usually two kinds of information given: that which concerns the company, and that which is about the people in the company. It is absolutely essential that the company information can be relied on: employees should believe what they read there rather than the grapevine. Certainly anything about the company which appears in the national or local press should be commented on. A question-and-answer section can be useful, and if questions are written to anyone in management, a careful answer should be given. (Anonymous letters here, as everywhere else, should be ignored.) Information about all locations should be included, as employees appreciate knowing what is happening in other places. Whether information about weddings, retirements, or competition successes should be mixed up with important company information is debatable. A full-size company newspaper will no doubt keep its company news separate from news about people, sports, and other activities as any other newspaper does.

If there is anything of great significance to communicate, a special edition will make an impact. Something like a merger, or a relocation plan, warrants this. If the producer of the company newspaper or newsletter can produce news instead of history, and give information before the grapevine flourishes, the company's version of events is more likely to be believed.

News dissemination

Some large companies attempt to give their employees some training in the wider aspects of business. Audio-visual programmes have been made to explain how the economy of this country works. It is very difficult to make such a programme acceptable both to manage-

ment and to the trade unions, but it has been done, and done success-
fully. It is believed that a knowledge of the economic 'facts of life'
will enable employees to take a more informed look at the problems
they and their companies face.

One large company, moving its central offices away from London,
set up an information room. This contained a comprehensive
amount of information for employees who would be moving to the
new location: housing, schools, shops, transport, employment for
other members of the family, recreational facilities; they had thought
of everything, and it was a magnificent achievement. The only drawback was that not many of the employees even knew it was there.

An information room would be a good investment in any company. In it employees would have access to a microcomputer, with
programs of the employees' handbook, the company pension
scheme, the share option scheme. There would be audio-visual
programmes of the company structure, other locations, the job-
evaluation and appraisal scheme, the company's products, and anything else the employees needed or wanted to know. There would
be a visual display unit which would show any up-to-the-minute
information. At certain hours, in their own time, employees could
use this room as a reference library.

The commonest way of communicating company information is
usually neglected, and often looks it: the notice-board or boards. A
small company will probably need only one or two, a large company
may need several more. It is absolutely necessary for management to
give attention to notice-boards. They must be properly sited, where
employees pass frequently and have room and light to see them. If
there is more than one, each should display a particular type of
information: situations vacant should not be mixed in with the
works dance and the first-aid class. One person must be in charge of
each notice-board, and only he should put up and take down notices.
'Take down' is very important; a torn poster announcing a Christmas
party looks very dreary in February. Only notices of an acceptable
standard should be displayed, and it must be the responsibility of
the person in charge to keep up this standard. If posters are to be
read, they must be eye-catching as well as properly designed. Something displayed too long will soon stop being seen; this is often the
fate of posters advocating health and safety at work. It should be the

pride of those who look after notice-boards that there are always people looking at them.

Solution:

Holiday Entitlement

For the eight National holidays and two additional holidays you will be paid as for ordinary 8-hour working days.

You must work the day before and the day after:
    (a) all National holidays;
    (b) if one or both additional holidays are added to a National holiday.

There are no conditions attached to:
    (a) taking one, or both, additional holidays, or
    (b) adding one, or both, additional holidays to your annual holiday.

The regulations as stated in 8(b) are ambiguous, as no distinction is made between National holidays, of which there will be only one in an annual holiday, and additional holidays which cannot be included in an annual holiday. Therefore:

You work the day after an annual holiday which includes a National holiday.

8 Seeing Is Believing

Visuals in communication

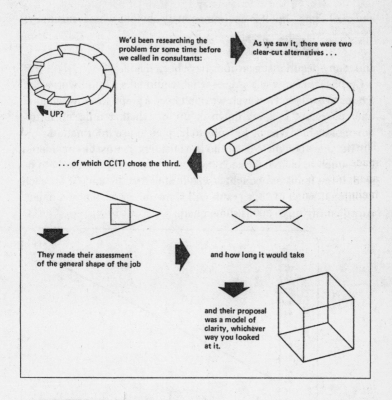

We'd been researching the problem for some time before we called in consultants:

As we saw it, there were two clear-cut alternatives . . .

UP?

. . . of which CC(T) chose the third.

They made their assessment of the general shape of the job

and how long it would take

and their proposal was a model of clarity, whichever way you looked at it.

. . . or is it?

Diagrams can be used, as can statistics, to mislead, but if they are used correctly, they help considerably to get the message across.

In situations where a language barrier must be overcome, symbols have been used for a very long time, and widely. The most usual are the variations on 'Ladies' and 'Gentlemen':

and road signs – but it is not immediately obvious what is meant by:

and many peculiar suggestions have been made.

Graphs can show at a glance what would take a lot of words and figures to explain. However, we don't need a graph to show whether unemployment is going down or up, or whether inflation is up, down or stable. We need graphs to help us to use information.

If items are bought to be resold in a business, it must be considered how much to charge for each item, and how many are likely to be sold. If the items are bought at £20 for the first 25, and £4 for each additional batch of 25, a graph will show the price of any number. Any quantity up to 300 is shown here:

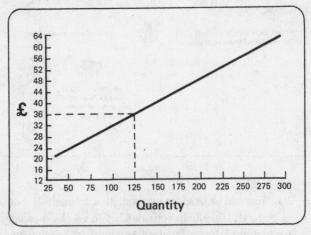

For example, 125 items will cost £36. This is the cost line.

On the basis that items sell better if they are cheap, the next thing is to find out how many must be sold at various prices to make a

profit. If one takes a low selling price, say 25p each, the income line
can be plotted: the seller will get £12.50 for 50, £25 for 100 and so on.
Where the cost line and the income line cross is the point at which
he will get his money back, that is the break-even point. At this price
(25p) he must sell about 175 items. (It must be taken into account
that no allowance has been made for selling costs, so enough profit
must be made to allow for these.)

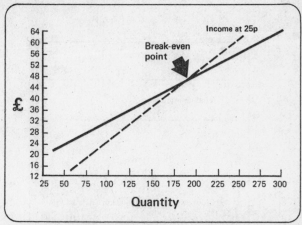

Supposing he sells at 40p per item, then the break-even point will
be 60, and sales over that, minus his expenses, will be profit.

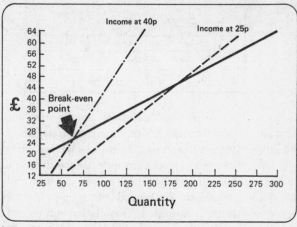

The great difficulty lies in estimating how many will be sold. Where a considerable amount of money is involved, market research will be necessary, as guessing is likely to lead to disaster.

In communicating financial information to employees, particularly the company's annual report and accounts, pie charts and cakes and bar and block charts have been used repeatedly.

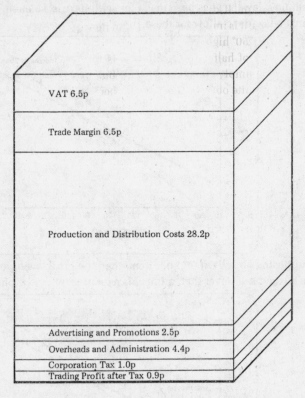

This diagram is intended to show where the 50p a customer pays for a packet of the company's product goes. It has two faults. First, the proportions are not correct. As the block is ten cm tall, each cm equals 5p. The top four blocks are approximately correct, but the 4.4 block should be almost 0.9 cm high instead of 0.6 cm and the bottom two about 0.2 cm each. The second fault is that a block is solid, and therefore volume is suggested. The relative volumes of the blocks are considerably different from the relative heights. These points may seem extremely trivial, but there is no purpose, except to mislead, in a bar or block chart which is not accurate.

The great difficulty comes when a very large amount has to be compared with a very small one. The obvious temptation is to abandon the scale, which defeats the whole object of the diagrammatic representation. If an expenditure of £50 million is shown by a bar 10 inches high, it is impossible to show an item of £100,000, as it would have to be 1/50″ high.

One way of half-coping with this is the magnifying-glass technique. It is simply changing the scale but, by drawing a magnifying glass, it is quite obvious that this has been done.

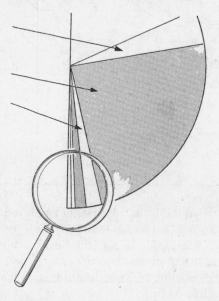

Some companies have substituted, in the place of charts in their annual reports, drawings of objects relevant to their products: beer mugs for breweries; rolls of paper for paper manufacturers; piles of cans for tin-can makers. These can make the production look very pleasant, but in the last resort the only thing that matters is the scale.

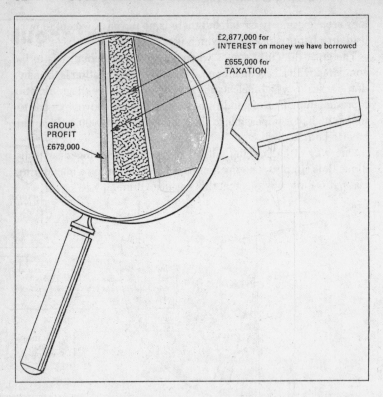

£2,877,000 for
INTEREST on money we have borrowed

£655,000 for
TAXATION

GROUP
PROFIT
£679,000

If in the annual report it is intended to tell the employees that the
amount the company pays in taxation would pay for X doctors or Y
nurses or Z dentists working for the National Health Service, there
is no point in adding to that information a drawing of a doctor, nurse
or dentist. This adds nothing to the understanding, as the readers
will know what each looks like.

Diagrams can be used to give a deal of financial information. The
example given on page 93 deals well with the relationship of added
value and profit.

Diagrams can also be used effectively for driving home economic
facts, and if employees can see and hear by way of audio-visual
programmes and can refresh their memories by reading a booklet,
there is a good chance of the message sticking. Good diagrams illustrating inflation are on page 94.

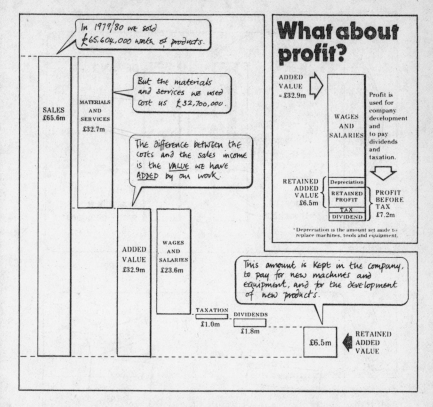

It has already been said that explaining pension schemes is an extremely difficult task, and that diagrams can help.

Although layout will be discussed in a later chapter, it is worth pointing out now that 'boxing' information, which might be considered to be turning it into a kind of diagram, helps in assimilation.

Consider whether it is easier to take in this:

The Plan Benefits

You will receive a pension from the day you retire until you die. After you retire, your pension will increase to help offset the effects of inflation. On retiring you can exchange part of your pension for a lump sum. After five years' service a Plan pension is preserved for you. With less than five years' service the government-guaranteed minimum pension is preserved. Death benefits are not preserved. If you die after you retire from the

Demand-pull inflation

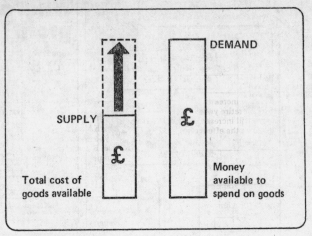

Cost-push inflation

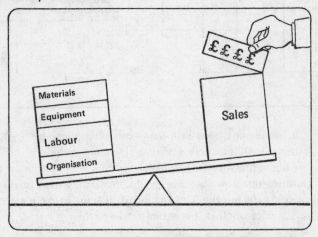

company your husband or wife will receive a pension. If you die in service or less than five years after you retire, a lump sum will be paid to someone nominated by you or to your estate. You can exchange part of your pension for a dependant's pension paid after you die.

or this:

THE PLAN BENEFITS

Retirement pension
You will receive a pension
from the day you retire
until you die.

Widow's or Widower's pension
If you die after you retire
from the company, your
husband or wife will receive
a pension.

Automatic increases
After you retire your
pension will increase to
help offset the effects
of inflation.

Death benefits
If you die in service or less
than 5 years after you retire,
a lump sum will be paid to
someone nominated by you
or to your estate.

Lump sum
On retiring you can
exchange part of your
pension for a lump sum.

Dependant's pension
You can exchange part of
your pension for a dependant's
pension, paid after you die.

Leaving service
After 5 years service, a
Plan pension is preserved for
you. With less than 5 years
service the government
guaranteed minimum pension
is preserved. Death benefits
are not preserved.

Most employees share in multi-million-pound pension funds which
pay out hundreds of thousands of pounds a year. But few know how
their fund works, how their benefits are safeguarded or even how
much their employers contribute towards pensions. The diagram at
the top of page 96 can help.

A spatial presentation can give essential information about a
pension scheme at a glance (see the diagram at the bottom of page
96).

How benefits are worked out can be explained by a guided
calculation (see page 97).

It takes great ingenuity to work out different ways of explaining
those items which appear in most pension schemes, for example the
average of the best three years' salaries, as in the diagram at the top
of page 97. That this diagram appears in many pensions booklets
really doesn't matter if it makes the point.

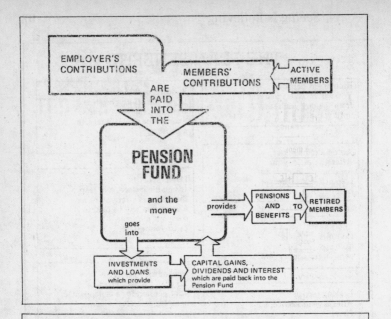

NEW PLAN

Under the new Plan you can choose:

either or

| FULL PENSION | | TAX-FREE LUMP SUM | + | REDUCED PENSION |

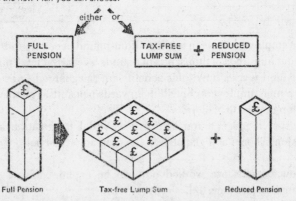

Full Pension   Tax-free Lump Sum   Reduced Pension

The amount of the lump sum is limited by Inland Revenue regulations.
The basic method used in calculating the lump sum will be:

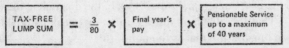

| TAX-FREE LUMP SUM | = | $\frac{3}{80}$ | × | Final year's pay | × | Pensionable Service up to a maximum of 40 years |

Your MAXIMUM LUMP SUM = 1½ times pay at the time of retirement.

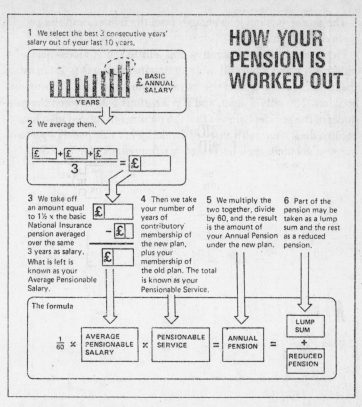

HOW YOUR PENSION IS WORKED OUT

1 We select the best 3 consecutive years' salary out of your last 10 years.

BASIC £ ANNUAL SALARY

YEARS

2 We average them.

$$\frac{£ + £ + £}{3} = £$$

3 We take off an amount equal to 1½ x the basic National Insurance pension averaged over the same 3 years as salary. What is left is known as your Average Pensionable Salary.

£ − £ = £

4 Then we take your number of years of contributory membership of the new plan, plus your membership of the old plan. The total is known as your Pensionable Service.

5 We multiply the two together, divide by 60, and the result is the amount of your Annual Pension under the new plan.

6 Part of the pension may be taken as a lump sum and the rest as a reduced pension.

The formula

$$\frac{1}{60} \times \text{AVERAGE PENSIONABLE SALARY} \times \text{PENSIONABLE SERVICE} = \text{ANNUAL PENSION} = \text{LUMP SUM} + \text{REDUCED PENSION}$$

Pictograms, diagrams using pictures to represent figures, seldom add much to their being understood. One, showing the increase in the number of passengers travelling by air from 1955 to 1975, gave the figures, followed by pictures of aeroplanes with little people standing by. The figures were:

1955	5,143,000
1965	20,642,000
1975	40,000,000

The increase is obvious enough from the figures, and the people were difficult to count.

Pictograms can be decorative and add to the attractiveness of a publication, and if they fill this function there is some point in using them. This is also true of the cartoons one often finds in pensions booklets. The only danger, and it is a serious one, is when the producer of the booklet believes that the picture of a retired man lounging in a deck chair with a tray of drinks by his side makes a piece of pension gobbledegook immediately comprehensible.

9 Sitting by Nellie

Communication in training

Training involves changing a person's behaviour, and there is a general implication that this change should be for the better. The top stars in all the great sports have their coaches and trainers; salesmen are trained; engineers are trained; doctors and nurses are trained; teachers are trained. No one wants a pet cat or dog unless it is 'house'-trained. Of course there is the other side: Fagin trained children to be more efficient thieves; saboteurs and terrorists are trained by the organizations using them.

In industry, training is usually taken to mean changing the behaviour of employees in work situations for the good of the company. 'Behaviour' in this context means 'the way a person performs' and is not particularly related to what is called 'good manners'. 'Behave yourself' – which most parents have said to their children at some time or other – is a silly request; the children were behaving, but badly instead of well. 'Stop behaving badly' would make more sense.

Training, then, is that art of teaching which modifies the behaviour of the taught. No doubt when some prehistoric man chipped flint with particularly good results, his mates gathered round and asked him to show them how to equal his performance. They watched and they tried to imitate. Sometimes the flint knapper said, 'No, not like that, watch me again,' and they did, and then they tried again with greater or less success. Certainly this is how the skill was passed from one generation to the next. And this is how skills were taught for tens of thousands of years. When training in industry became important and new techniques were developed, this old-fashioned method was called, in a derogatory way, 'sitting by Nellie'.

What, if anything, is wrong with sitting by Nellie? The honest answer is 'Nothing much', if Nellie is very good at her job, can both demonstrate well and communicate well, as there will usually be questions which require answers, and 'showing how' is not always as easy as it seems. One drawback is that Nellie will not be able to get on with her job at the usual speed, as some time will be taken up with demonstrations and explanations.

Difficulties begin if Nellie isn't quite as good as she might be: perhaps she goes a long way round to perform some tasks. Because she is so good, maybe she has added to her job mystique by putting in a bit of dressing-up. In one vehicle bodybuilding factory, an operation in which a hammer and tacks were used had one interesting feature: the hammer was thrown up and caught again. It transpired that this had no function, but someone in high spirits had started it, it looked good, and it was perpetuated . . . and it wasted quite a bit of time. In the same factory, a considerable number of tacks were put in the mouth before each task was begun. Each tack was turned round in turn by the tongue so that the head stuck out between the lips, ready to be taken out of the mouth to be used. This was highly dangerous, and inevitably tacks were swallowed, but it was regarded as part of the task, and newcomers followed the rest. There was also a belief that only other people swallowed tacks.

Real interest in training, particularly as a communication exercise, appeared in the UK in the 1960s, and from two directions: first, the development of teaching machines and other self-instruction devices; and secondly, the setting up of the Industrial Training Boards resulting from the Industrial Training Act. Companies had to pay levies to their particular ITB, and they received grants if their training was considered adequate.

One of the difficulties encountered was that there were lamentably few trainers, so that people who had been proved to be good at their jobs suddenly found themselves turned into teachers. Being good at doing something does not necessarily mean that one is good at teaching someone else; often the reverse, as the difficulties cannot be seen. Poor Nellie suddenly found herself, not with just one learner sitting by her side, but planning a course, facing a class, and being made responsible for getting the students through their tests. The trainers needed to be trained in training.

This was the climate in which the research, which had been done on training, had to be tried out. The dogs had salivated; the rats had run their mazes; the pigeons had chosen their boxes. Now, the whole of UK industry was wanting to know more about training.

Self-, or programmed, instruction grew out of animal conditioning experiments, by which animals were rewarded for making the correct response, and the reward 'reinforced' the response. In the early 1960s, programmed instruction seemed to be a very hopeful technique for training, but it proved to be a great disappointment. There were several reasons for this. One was that enthusiasm for the new technique led to the production of a great number of very bad and very boring programs, and the technique itself became discredited. Another was that programmed instruction is very difficult to write and therefore good courses were rare and very expensive to produce. Although we hear little about it now, programmed instruction still has a very definite place in training, and this is discussed in Chapter 10.

Only a few generalizations can be made about training in industry. What is common to training a lathe operator, a brewery drayman, an insurance salesman, a shop assistant and computer programmer? There are an enormous number and variety of jobs and, within each of these jobs, a number of tasks. There is no agreement about definitions, but these have been found useful:

job everything a person does to earn a living

task part of a job

If the job is 'dentist', some of the tasks are: filling teeth, crowning teeth, extracting teeth, measuring for dentures.

'Task' itself needs defining; it can be considered to be a self-contained piece of work producing a result.

Some jobs are so simple that they consist of only one task, for example refilling the shelves in a supermarket. To communicate to the trainee just once how this is done is probably enough, although there will be procedures which must be carried out correctly: how to collect the goods; where to take them from; how and where to record what has been taken; how to place them in the right positions. It is not difficult perhaps, but it has to be done correctly by all concerned, or chaos would result. One way of communicating what has to be done is to demonstrate, and say, 'This is how you do it.' Another

way is to tell the trainee to watch Nellie. A third way is to explain
what has to be done, why it has to be done that particular way, and
to give the trainee a card or piece of paper on which the instructions
are clearly set out, in the right order.

Exercise: You can decide which method is most likely to produce
the required result. Write your comments and see if you
agree with those of the author which will be found at the
end of the chapter.

Some jobs are so complicated that they take years to master, for
example interpreting the orthopaedic surgeon's prescription and
measuring for, and giving instructions for the manufacture of, surgi-
cal appliances. Here, an integrated course of theory and practical
work is necessary. The great difficulty is the integration, or students
will be left with a mass of information about anatomy and physiology, congenital defects, the rheumatic illnesses and other relevant
conditions, which they will try to relate to their work in orthopaedic
clinics and in the factories where the appliances are made.

The setting up of the ITBs gave training a new importance, and
the establishment of 'best practices' was invaluable. Having established a 'best practice', it had to be perpetuated. So we come back
to communication: what was the best way of communicating how
to perform a task? One way of doing this served a double purpose:
it was the production of manuals which acted as structured *aides-
mémoire* to the trainers, and also as action guides for the trainees.

The production of these manuals involved breaking down each
task into a logical sequence, and illustrating how to carry this out.
So often we come back to this 'logical sequence', not only in training
but in any instructions, particularly user manuals.

In training for simple jobs, it must be decided which is the appropriate method, and the appropriate medium overall. In training for
complex jobs, it must be decided which is the appropriate method
and medium *for each task*:

> sitting by Nellie
>
> classroom instruction
>
> self-instruction

Sitting by Nellie we know about. Self-instruction will be considered in detail in the next chapter.

Classroom instruction can consist of talks, demonstrations and audio-visual programmes of various sorts; but, whatever the medium, its value is only as good as the message, and the message is communicating what has to be done. Obviously demonstrations will be important, so will watching the trainees' attempts and diagnosing what is wrong, what could be improved, and what is as good as it can be. We are told that practice makes perfect, which is certainly not true; practice only improves performance if it is carefully monitored so that faults are eradicated. Otherwise, repetition only perpetuates the errors.

Many companies miss a golden opportunity by not providing induction training. Often all that a new employee receives is a letter of appointment and an employees' handbook, which may be largely incomprehensible. Most employees would like to know something about the company they have joined. Does it exist on its own? Is it part of a large group of companies, perhaps multinational? Who runs the company? Where are its various locations? This is where a good audio-visual programme can prove useful, to communicate company information to new employees, even to one new employee, to make him feel that he is being introduced to his new company, and that he matters enough to be told about it.

One area which has received a deal of attention lately is sales and marketing training. It may be that this is considered more important than other training because selling is obviously vital to a company's success. In one recently published book on the subject, over 300 pages long, no mention is made of one extremely important aspect of selling: product knowledge. Some salesmen have extremely complicated products to sell: scientific instruments; insurance; pharmaceutical products. They can only sell properly if they know all about their product and can answer any questions which prospective buyers may ask, and this often involves knowing much more than just a description of the product. Either the salesman must know or he must have a sales aid.

Consider the pharmaceutical company's salesman who has to persuade doctors and consultants to prescribe his company's products. Suppose he is hoping to sell a new drug for arthritis sufferers. First he must know enough anatomy and physiology to be able to discuss the rheumatic diseases with experts. He must know enough pharmacology to talk about what the new drug can do, and how it does it. He must be able to answer questions about the clinical trials which have been conducted. He must be able to compare his company's products with those of other companies which probably make the same claims. He must be aware of the side-effects of the new drug, and those of his competitors' products. How can all this information be communicated to him without taking him off the road for a long time? The answer is by some self-instructional means, possibly a programmed text, to be discussed in Chapter 10; possibly a video cassette which he can watch and listen to at home.

See page 105 for an illustration taken from a programmed text on the respiratory system.

Representatives were selling a numerical control system designed for machine tools. It was a modular system made up of a set of basic hardware and various options which a customer could add. The problem facing the salesmen was that some alternatives or options were incompatible, and they did not know enough electronics to distinguish these. The solution was a diagrammatic guide which distinguished between 'must have' and 'can have', and between 'ors' and 'ands', and which could also serve as an order form, a tick being put in the box against the option chosen (see the illustrative diagram on page 106).

An important decision which has to be made is whether conventional training is necessary or whether it is better to produce performance aids. No one would be happy having a tooth extracted by a dentist who was holding a manual entitled 'Self-instruction in Dentistry' in one hand and a pair of forceps in the other, but there are circumstances where training is wasteful and virtually useless. If there is a very high staff turnover, a job aid which can be given to any newcomer and which communicates exactly what is to be done is obviously more sensible to avoid perpetual training. Training for a situation which occurs infrequently or hardly ever is also wasteful if a job aid can be produced, as training will soon be forgotten. A good example is that of the continuous furnace which occasionally becomes dangerous, to the extent that an explosion is possible, and a warning sounds. This very rarely happens, but if it does there must

8.2 THE MECHANICS OF RESPIRATION; RESPIRATORY VOLUMES; CONTROL OF RESPIRATION

The Mechanics of Respiration

The lungs are contained within a closed cavity – the thorax.

The inside of the thorax is lined with two layers of thin moist membrane, the pleura.

The pressure between the two pleura is a few mm of Hg below atmospheric pressure.

The thorax is enclosed by

- the diaphragm
- the sternum
- the ribs and intercostal muscles
- the vertebral column at the back.

At inspiration, air is drawn into the lungs as a result of an increase in size of the thoracic cavity due to active contraction of:

(1) the diaphragm   and   (2) the intercostal muscles

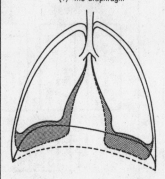 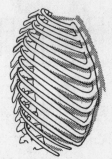

Expiration of air is due to the decrease in size of the cavity when the diaphragm and intercostal muscles relax.

In normal breathing, there are 16–18 inspirations and expirations each minute.

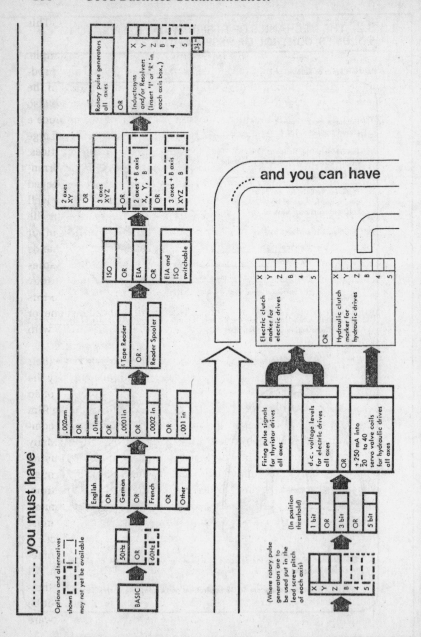

be an easy-to-follow guide to what to do to prevent disaster. This procedure is described in Chapter 12.

There are situations in which training is comparatively simple. The very successful pharmaceutical salesman who has a new product to sell only needs to have communicated to him details of the new drug in order to sell it with his customary skill. There are also situations in which training is not simple and will not produce a solution. One area where this is true is in safety training. Large amounts of money can be spent in training workers in safe practices; in emphasizing the desirability of safe working; in showing horrendous films of what happens if the safe-working rules are disobeyed – and still the accident rate stays unacceptably high. This can well be because it is considered cowardly to put the guards on the machine or to wear the safety goggles. In one sawmill the author visited, it was a matter of pride for the workers to hold up both hands to show how many fingers, or parts of fingers, were missing. Ladies with beautiful hair dislike hiding it all inside a cap, although they may know about scalping. There are two possible solutions to this problem: to change attitudes, which is difficult, but can be done; or to keep such a watch that to break the safety rules and get away with it is impossible.

In one airline, loaders were extremely careless in driving their fork-lift trucks, and accidents were frequent, involving not only the loaders, but the aircraft. Driving a fork-lift truck into the side of an aeroplane is good for neither man nor plane. A safety training film was produced which caught the imagination of the loaders, communicating the problem by relating it to their own experience. Many of them knew people who had invested a lot of money in buying a taxi, and they could appreciate what it would mean if, through someone's careless driving, the taxi was off the road for some time, resulting in loss of earnings. After seeing this film, the improvement in their performance was spectacular. Simply reiterating 'You must not drive your trucks into our planes' would have had no effect.

Training schools and departments tend to be full of gadgets, sometimes resembling an audio-visual equipment dealer's showroom. All this hardware no doubt suggests keeping-up-to-date-with-all-that-is-new, and an aura of corresponding efficiency which may not be true at all. Much more important than the hardware is the software that it reproduces. This is not intended to deprecate the use of audio-visual equipment, which can be extremely effective; it is simply to point out that with audio-visual equipment, as with computers, garbage in = garbage out.

There are three possible routes for obtaining training programmes: to buy them 'off the shelf'; to make them oneself; to have them tailor-made by specialists. This does sound rather like buying a suit, and the results are very similar: a suit 'off the peg' will sometimes fit very well, quite often fit more or less well, and occasionally fit not at all. If you run it up yourself, the result will depend on how good you are at making suits; and if you go to Savile Row, it will fit very well indeed, probably perfectly.

There are some extremely good ready-made audio-visual training programmes obtainable but, like the suit, they seldom fit the particular communication situation exactly. (There are also a lot of extremely bad programmes.) However good the photography or the cartoons may be, it is the *message* that matters. It is not enough that trainees have been entertained for a quarter of an hour. Something should have been communicated to them which will change or modify their behaviour in the way that was intended.

To make an audio-visual training programme oneself does depend entirely on competence. To make acceptable overhead projector transparencies and provide the audio part oneself is different from making a more or less permanent and fixed audio-visual programme. Overhead projector transparencies are discussed in Chapter 13.

There are a number of specialist companies with very good reputations for making audio-visual training programmes. The programme makers must know exactly what your message is to be. They must then devise a way of communicating that message so that it is acceptable. This is where their very special skill lies. Part of that skill lies in knowing exactly what questions to ask, in order to extract the correct information. They then must produce the programme. So there is a double communication exercise here; in the example quoted: from airline to film maker, from film maker to fork-lift truck drivers.

Training is an immensely important part of communication in business, yet since the 1960s little attention seems to have been paid to it except in the fields of sales and marketing. Perhaps it is believed that with the ever-increasing development of technology, it is no longer necessary. There is a lot more which needs to be communicated, however, than simply which button to press.

To state that the best way to train supermarket shelf-fillers depends on how well the three methods are carried out may seem like sitting on the fence, but it is probably true. The first method (being given a demonstration) depends on how good the demonstration is. But the trainee has only memory to rely on afterwards. Sitting by Nellie can also be effective, if Nellie is good at her job and the 'sitting' can go on until the trainee is competent. The third way (an explanation followed by written instructions), again depends on how good the explanation and instructions are. The great advantage of written instructions is that they can be referred to at any time and also be passed on to new trainees.

10 Teach Yourself

Self-instruction and communication

There was great enthusiasm for programmed instruction in the 1960s; it was to be the panacea for all training ills. That it didn't turn out like that we know. In its heyday it was taken very seriously indeed, and many learned books and articles were written about it. It was based on scientific research which made it very respectable. What is programmed instruction?

Programmed instruction is sometimes called self-instruction. It really should be called 'programmed self-instruction'. It is also called programmed learning. Whether it is instruction or learning depends on whether it is being considered from the point of view of the learner or the teacher. The important word is 'programmed'. The material to be taught or learnt is arranged in a series of steps, each of which contains the correct amount of new information that can be absorbed. After each step the learner is questioned; when he gets the correct answer, he moves on to the next step.

There are verbal conventions attached to programmed instruction. It is usual to spell 'program' the American way, which is also the convention for computing. A program is called a 'programmed text'. Each piece of information is called a 'frame', and the answers to the questions are known as 'responses'. There are 'copy frames', in which the answers to the questions can be copied from the text with or without being understood; and 'gruyère cheese' frames, when a sentence of the text is copied out with one or more gaps, and each gap has to be filled in.

If this is part of a piece of information:

> The whole of the gastro-intestinal tract has a very rich blood supply which carries away the absorbed products of digestion.

and the question is:

> What carries away the absorbed products of digestion?

the answer can simply be copied:

> The blood supply of the gastro-intestinal tract.

This is a copy frame, and useless. Equally useless would be

> The —— supply carries away the absorbed products of digestion. Fill in the gap.

This is a gruyère cheese frame. Perhaps the existence of copy and gruyère cheese frames indicates why programmed instruction did not live up to its promise.

There are two ways of constructing a program: in the first, called 'linear', the student works straight through each frame in turn, referring back if he gets the answer wrong. In the second, called 'branching', if the student gets the answer wrong he works through additional frames until he can get the right answer. Branching programs are useful if the students are of various abilities or at different stages of knowledge. These differences must not be very great, or the program would have to be enormous.

The scientific and empirical background to programmed instruction came from animal conditioning experiments. If a hungry animal performed a task satisfactorily (a rat running a maze correctly, for example) and it was rewarded by being fed, then it was more likely to repeat that correct performance. In jargon terms, its response was reinforced. On the other hand, if no reward was given, there was no incentive for repeating the correct performance. The theoretical basis for programmed instruction was this reinforcement. B. F. Skinner, a Harvard psychologist, was the pioneer. He applied his findings to human learning, and made the assumption that people wanted success, and then wrote teaching programs, giving a small piece of information and asking for a response, such as filling in a blank. He supposed that getting the answer right was a reinforcement. These programs showed that Skinner had discovered something, as his method took 70 per cent of the normal time to teach 90 per cent of a given group to score 90 per cent in an examination. (The programs were not teaching complex material.)

The advantage of programmed teaching is that the information can be gathered for the needs of a particular group of people. Their existing knowledge can be discovered, and the reason for their wanting to know, and how much they need to know, can be found out.

The advantages of programmed learning are that the learner can work when and where and for how long a time he finds convenient. No one will see how well or how badly he does. If the program is well constructed it will be interesting and he will be aware of the progress he is making.

Before material can be programmed there are important decisions to be made:

> what is the information which has to be communicated and for what purpose?

> what does the person to be taught already know?

> how can the material be processed in a logical way?

> what size should each step in teaching be?

> what questions will test what the learner has taken in?

In any training programme of any kind, the first essential is to decide what has to be taught, and why. It may be the anatomy and physiology of the digestive system, say. The reason for teaching it could be that a pharmaceutical company's salesmen are introducing a new indigestion tablet, and, as they have to talk to doctors, they must be able to discuss the digestive system, how it can go wrong, and the action of the tablet. If this particular company's representatives are all qualified pharmacists, the level of existing knowledge will be high, and little basic explanation will be needed.

It used to be the custom to start a program with a test, known as the pre-test, to find out how many questions the learner could answer, and end with the same test (only it was now the post-test), to find out how much the learner's performance had improved. This procedure would make sense only in very simple programs.

The programmer (we call the programmer 'he', but a good programmer is equally likely to be 'she') must make himself totally familiar with the subject; select what is required for this particular purpose; arrange it logically; and divide it into self-contained 'steps'.

2.1. Anatomy

The digestive system consists of:

(1) the alimentary canal

a long, continuous, tube passing from the mouth to the anus containing the following parts:

(2) associated organs:

the three salivary glands

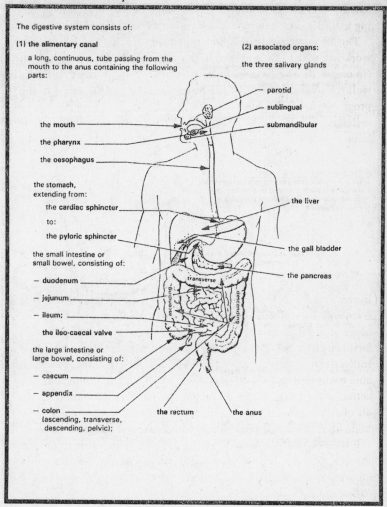

- the mouth
- the pharynx
- the oesophagus

the stomach, extending from:
- the cardiac sphincter
- to:
- the pyloric sphincter

the small intestine or small bowel, consisting of:
- duodenum
- jejunum
- ileum;
- the ileo-caecal valve

the large intestine or large bowel, consisting of:
- caecum
- appendix
- colon (ascending, transverse, descending, pelvic);

parotid
sublingual
submandibular

the liver

the gall bladder

the pancreas

transverse
ascending
descending

the rectum   the anus

He must then devise questions which require the learner to work on the material rather than copy it. This sounds easy, but in fact it is a very difficult process indeed, particularly devising testing questions.

2.2. Functions

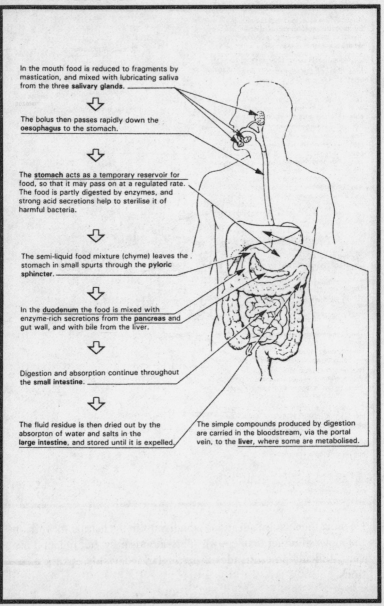

In the mouth food is reduced to fragments by mastication, and mixed with lubricating saliva from the three **salivary glands**.

The bolus then passes rapidly down the **oesophagus** to the stomach.

The **stomach** acts as a temporary reservoir for food, so that it may pass on at a regulated rate. The food is partly digested by enzymes, and strong acid secretions help to sterilise it of harmful bacteria.

The semi-liquid food mixture (chyme) leaves the stomach in small spurts through the **pyloric sphincter**.

In the **duodenum** the food is mixed with enzyme-rich secretions from the **pancreas** and gut wall, and with bile from the liver.

Digestion and absorption continue throughout the **small intestine**.

The fluid residue is then dried out by the absorpton of water and salts in the **large intestine**, and stored until it is expelled.

The simple compounds produced by digestion are carried in the bloodstream, via the portal vein, to the **liver**, where some are metabolised.

3.1. Fertilisation and implantation

About 300 million spermatozoa are ejaculated by the male into the female genital tract. About 1 million of these swim through the cervix, where the mucus is thinned by oestrogenic activity during ovulation. A few hours later a few hundred spermatozoa reach the uterine tube. The spermatozoa have a useful life span of about 48 hours.

The ovum comes to lie in the uterine tube within an hour or so of ovulation. It remains able to be fertilised for about 48 hours.

The ovum is surrounded by a corona of small cells and by a thin membrane, the **zona pellucida**. The zona allows one, and only one, spermatozoon to penetrate it. This fuses with the ovum and its nuclear material swells. It joins with the female nucleus to restore the usual double chromosome complement. This set of chromosomes contains all the information for the production of a new individual, combining the maternal and paternal characteristics in a unique way.

The fertilised egg divides within the zona to form two, four, eight, sixteen and eventually a ball of cells with a central fluid-filled cavity. This is the **blastocyst**.

The blastocyst is gradually carried along the uterine tube, by peristalsis, to the uterine cavity where 5–7 days later it implants, usually in the upper uterus.

The zona prevents premature implantation of the blastocyst into the uterine tube, and then soon disintegrates.

The implanted blastocyst digests the endometrium it lies on and sinks into the thick, fleshy tissue to become completely buried.

The outer layer of the blastocyst, the **chorion**, invades the endometrium with finger-like projections called **villi**.

It absorbs nutrients and secretes the hormone human choriogonadotrophin (HCG).

HCG is a powerful hormone which imitates LH, maintaining the corpus luteum and preventing menstruation. (It can be readily detected in blood and urine and forms the basis of pregnancy testing.)

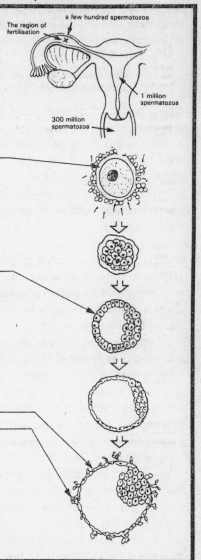

a few hundred spermatozoa

The region of fertilisation

1 million spermatozoa

300 million spermatozoa

A page from a self-instructional course on anatomy and physiology is reproduced on page 115. The question in Test 3 demands that the learner takes in the material and processes it, rather than simply copying out the answer. Of course, nothing must be asked which cannot be answered from the information supplied.

Test Three

1. Why would it be true to say that the zona pellucida functions solely as a control?

One of the most important principles insisted on by the pioneers of programmed instruction is that of validation. It is presumptuous for a writer to think that he knows the intelligence, educational standard, knowledge, and ability to assimilate information of any group of people. A certain amount of this can be found out by investigation, but it is unwise to take anything for granted. For example, some pharmaceutical companies employ only trained pharmacists as representatives; others ask for a proven record in sales, often in a completely different industry in an entirely different field. A great number of highly educated people are completely ignorant about finance, even its terminology, and, in spite of their general level of education, must be treated as ignorant in this particular subject. A distinction must be made between 'not knowing' and 'stupid', which some people fail to make.

When a program has to be written, as much information as possible must be collected about the students, and then certain assumptions have to be made. The only test of a program's effectiveness is whether it teaches what it is supposed to teach to the people for whom it is written. It is obviously wasteful to produce a whole program and then try it out to see if it works. The usual practice is for a certain amount to be written and then tried out on a representative sample of people. These guinea-pigs are encouraged to think aloud as they work through the frames, commenting on and criticizing the text, the questions, and the general presentation in some detail. It is a salutary experience for the writer to find out that he's got it wrong; but at least this way he'll know *how* he's got it wrong and will be able to make the necessary adjustments. The great difficulty is to get the pace right. Too slow is boring, too fast makes the program difficult to work through. 'Slow' means presenting the material in too small steps, and 'fast' in too big steps. Early programs were very slow indeed, and so were some produced in the 1960s, and this helped to give the technique a bad name.

There are several other reasons why programmed instruction went out of favour. It is a difficult and time-consuming job to write a program well; therefore, good programs are expensive. To be cost-effective, a program must be used by a considerable number of people. (However, it should be remembered that they need not all be studying at the same time. The program could be an introduction to something which all newcomers must be familiar with and which, over a period, would save a lot of training time.) Opposition to self-instruction is expressed by many trainers who feel that their image as purveyors of instruction is being destroyed. It has also been used in inappropriate situations.

The theoretical basis was reinforcement. Get it right and you will be rewarded, so you'll get it right again. What is the equivalent reward, of the food given to the rats for running a maze correctly, for students getting an answer right? In the beginning there was an assumption that this was reward enough. But, as one of the pioneers of programmed instruction pointed out, merely being right is stunningly boring. Good programmed texts are amazingly efficient. The desire to get to know, or motivation, is the most important factor in the success of self-instruction. Imagine that pharmaceutical company's salesman who has to sell a new indigestion tablet. Any time spent off the road is expensive to his company – and to him if he works on a commission basis – but he has to learn all about the body's digestive system, the pharmacology of the tablet, and rival companies' similar products, which could be a daunting prospect. He must be able to talk on those subjects on equal terms with doctors, or they will send him away with a flea in his ear. He wants to know, he wants to know quickly, and he wants to take as little time off the road as possible.

A good program would solve his problem. He could work through it when and where it suited him. If he got the answers to the questions right first time, he would be pleased. If he didn't, he could go back and find out why he was wrong. Equally well, he could cheat. He could look up the answers and then work out why they were right. It has been proved that students in many circumstances learn just as well if they cheat as if they don't. This would not be so if they just looked up the answers but didn't bother to find out why they were correct.

Motivation is of vital importance in any learning situation; the stronger the motivation, the more obstacles will be overcome. But, there comes a point when even strong motivation peters out if the obstacles are too great. A well-constructed self-instruction course with few difficulties and with guaranteed success keeps the motivation going. It is obvious that self-instruction works only if the program is properly constructed: the programming is all-important.

It is difficult to train in a conventional way for a situation which may happen some time in the future. An international banking group wished to train its potential managers in the granting of commercial loans. The problem was that the training would have to be carried out in the field, and that covered several continents. It might be some years after leaving this country before the manager would have reached such a position of seniority that he had to decide the credit-worthiness of potential borrowers. The training was to be aimed at improving the manager's judgement of when and how much to lend. It was believed by some in the group that judgement was something you had or hadn't – and if you hadn't, you couldn't be taught. One senior official of the bank said that his whiskers twitched the moment a customer who was a bad risk entered the room.

A programmed text was designed to introduce the trainee to the basic concepts and take him through all the stages of assessing an applicant for a loan. Practical examples of increasing complexity were repeatedly referred to at progressively higher levels. The program was accompanied by a manual which the trainee could use after he had worked through the program, as a performance aid to help him in his job as long as he needed it. Ten years after the program was devised the bank was still using it, an indication of its success.

Skinner presented his early programs in simple machines which displayed one frame at a time, and moved on to the next when the right answer was given. This was to prevent students from cheating, which has since been discovered not to matter. Teaching machines, which rarely worked efficiently, became popular for a very short time. Most programs were printed and the responses were written.

This is still the case, but now that microcomputers are small, easily portable and cheap, there may be a revived interest in programmed learning. Unlike the early teaching machines, these extremely sophisticated pieces of equipment do not break down, and people are fascinated by using them.

One of the drawbacks of branching programs when they are printed is their size. Yet they are necessary if there is a discrepancy in the knowledge of the various people who will use them: definitions can be included and extra information can be given. If the program is put into a computer, size doesn't matter, and, as it doesn't, the student can be more in control of his learning, and he can go directly to the part of the program he wants. In fact, the student and the computer carry on a conversation. Performance can be scored with or without the knowledge of the student, which can be useful to a trainer.

One of the drawbacks of using a microcomputer for self-instruction is that the facilities for producing illustrations are limited. Graphs and charts and simple line-drawings are possible, but not the kind of illustrations which would be needed, say, in a medical program. This problem can be overcome by using a book containing the illustrations alongside the program.

The most splendid teaching machines combine computer with audio-visual technology and there are many devices for student interaction, including indicating choice by touching the screen with a light pen. These are referred to in Chapter 13, on audio-visual aids.

The smallest computers are bulky compared to manuals, and they need a source of power. A book can go with the student, whereas he has to go to the computer or teaching machine.

No amount of high technology will compensate for a badly produced program. Writing programmed texts is difficult enough, and combining this with a knowledge of a computer language (probably only Basic, but it still has to be learnt) and all the possibilities in the presentation of the material, is a formidable task. But there is no doubt that sophisticated teaching machines offer a great deal more than programmed texts, and most people find them fascinating to use.

There are plenty of ready-made programs on the market, ranging from texts to those which are audio-visual and interactive. As has been said when discussing training, these can fit superbly, more or less, or not at all. Ideally they should be produced to exact needs. Some companies which sell off-the-shelf programs will add to them to suit a customer's particular requirements. For example, suppose there is a very good program on the digestive system; it could have added to it a further section on the pharmaceutical company's new indigestion tablet.

It will be a great pity if programmed instruction does not enjoy a rebirth.

11 Yes or No

Algorithms as a technique of communication

In 1966, two very different problems in industry which appeared to be training problems were solved in very similar ways. One was concerned with fault-finding and servicing a new portable electric typewriter which was being sold over a wide geographical area. The other was concerned with preventing corrosion in the boiler of a chemical factory.

The problem in the first example was how to train service men in all those parts of the world where the typewriter was being sold, so that they could cope with faults as soon as they began to appear. Obviously, formal training was out of the question, so training consultants were asked for suggestions. There were two communication-at-a-distance difficulties; the first was to tell all the service men how the typewriter worked, as it differed from the company's earlier models; the other was how to find the likely and most frequent faults and put them right.

The first difficulty was solved by producing a manual which had a line-drawing of each part to show exactly how it worked. There was also a drawing for each part showing its place in the whole mechanism (see page 122). The second difficulty was solved by producing a manual of fault-finding algorithms with the remedies (see the diagram on page 123).

As this all took place twenty years ago, the use of algorithms in an industrial training situation was virtually unknown.

The second problem was solved at exactly the same time. The boiler which provided steam for a process plant was looked after by supervisors. The water which was turned into steam came from a nearby river. This was a highly industrial area, and the river water was polluted by the waste from various other plants. The chemical

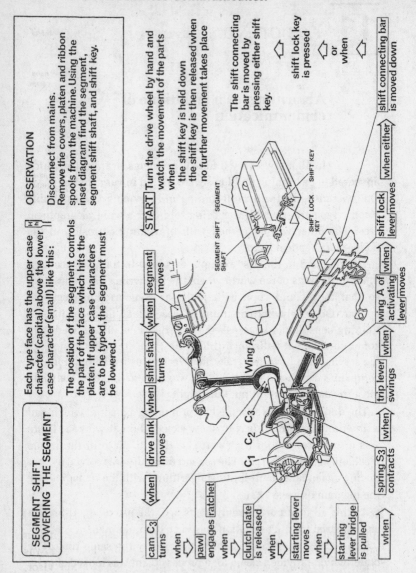

composition of the water changed according to how this waste changed, and could vary from one shift to another. Untreated water would cause the boiler to corrode and eventually explode, so it was

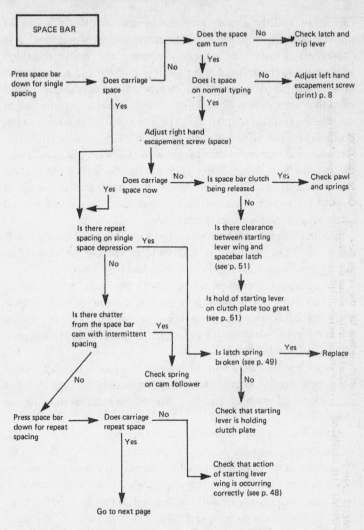

put through a treatment plant where various measures were taken to counteract the impurities. Twice a day the intake water was sampled in the laboratory and a report was given to the supervisor, who then decided what treatment was necessary. Unfortunately, wrongly treated water had the same effect as untreated water: corrosion which eventually led to boiler replacement, which was very expensive, and the shut-down time needed for this to be carried out was even more expensive. The management of the plant was concerned because the supervisors were not doing their job adequately, so the training department was asked to arrange a course in water chemistry in order that the supervisors should understand what they were doing. This, they decided, would take some four to six weeks of full-time instruction. This couldn't be arranged, so the problem was passed to consultants. Again, there were two difficulties: how could supervisors be taught water chemistry without a full-time course; and, if they didn't want all this information (which was reasonable, as water treatment was only a small part of the job of controlling a very complex plant), was there any other way of improving the supervisors' performance?

The first difficulty was overcome by producing a self-instructional course in water treatment which could be worked through at the supervisors' own speed and when they had time for it.

The second difficulty was solved by producing an algorithm (see page 125) which the supervisor could work through quickly and reach the correct decision. This algorithm was always available when it had to be used as it was printed on the back of the laboratory's analysis report form.

The supervisors were also given a half-day course on why correct water treatment is so important; they were made familiar with the basic chemical symbols; and they were given practice in using the algorithm.

Algorithms have been written about here but not so far defined. Various attempts have been made to produce an adequate definition. The word comes from theoretical mathematics, where it means an exact prescription for solving a problem. One definition is 'a sequence of questions logically structured so that they go from the most general to the most specific, arranged so that only the most relevant to a specific case need be read'. In the last two decades, algorithms have become a tool for enabling people to solve problems as well as computers. People can work through algorithms automatically and, so long as they understand the language, particularly the technical terms or jargon, no wider knowledge of the problem is necessary for a solution to be reached.

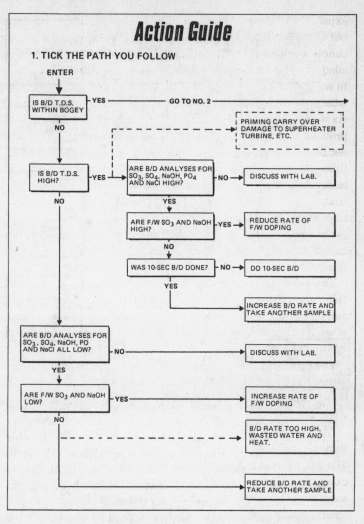

Action Guide

1. TICK THE PATH YOU FOLLOW

ENTER

IS B/D T.D.S. WITHIN BOGEY — YES ——— GO TO NO. 2 ——————→

PRIMING CARRY OVER DAMAGE TO SUPERHEATER TURBINE, ETC.

IS B/D T.D.S. HIGH? — YES → ARE B/D ANALYSES FOR SO₃, SO₄, NaOH, PO₄ AND NaCl HIGH? — NO → DISCUSS WITH LAB.

NO

YES

ARE F/W SO₃ AND NaOH HIGH? — YES → REDUCE RATE OF F/W DOPING

NO

WAS 10-SEC B/D DONE? — NO → DO 10-SEC B/D

YES

INCREASE B/D RATE AND TAKE ANOTHER SAMPLE

ARE B/D ANALYSES FOR SO₃, SO₄, NaOH, PO AND NaCl ALL LOW? — NO ————→ DISCUSS WITH LAB.

YES

ARE F/W SO₃ AND NaOH LOW? — YES → INCREASE RATE OF F/W DOPING

NO

B/D RATE TOO HIGH. WASTED WATER AND HEAT.

REDUCE B/D RATE AND TAKE ANOTHER SAMPLE

On page 126 is reproduced part of an algorithm to determine the rate which a shift worker should be paid. Here, it is necessary to read only three out of the nine boxes, and the important changeover situation is dealt with first. The need to read only those sentences relevant to a particular case is obviously important, and proceeding from the most general to the most specific may be important. For

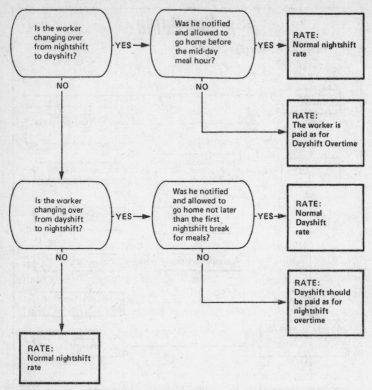

example, if the rules for membership of a society are different for men and women, the obvious start is 'Are you a man [or woman]?' as neither need bother with what refers only to the other. In other circumstances, however, it may be better to start with what happens most often. This can be the case with a machine fault-finding algorithm, when experience provides a knowledge of fault frequency; the algorithm on page 127 is an example of this kind.

Some algorithms have instructions as well as questions.

Some people would call the pay algorithm a 'logical tree', as it has no instructions, and the car starter one an algorithm proper. Such distinctions seem to have no point, as algorithms can have various forms. Perhaps the most satisfactory definition is: a means of reaching a decision by considering only those factors which are relevant to that decision.

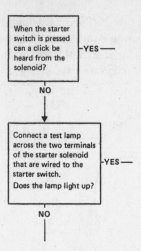

We have seen parts of flow-chart algorithms. Another way of presenting them is in list-structure form. Here is another version of the shift workers' pay algorithm.

(1) Is the worker changing over from nightshift to dayshift?
    YES Go to (3)
    NO Go to (2)
(2) Is the worker changing over from dayshift to nightshift?
    YES Go to (4)
    NO Normal nightshift rate
(3) Was he notified and allowed to go home before the midday mealtime?
    YES Normal nightshift rate
    NO Dayshift overtime rate
(4) Was he notified and allowed to go home not later than the first nightshift break for meals?
    YES Normal dayshift rate
    NO Nightshift overtime rate

This looks more familiar than questions in boxes, and so some people prefer it.

For those people who cannot resist reading any print in sight, there can be a compulsion to read right through an algorithm instead of using it. One way of defeating this is to make a device which displays only one question at a time. Wheels and slides have been used; this is one advantage of using a microcomputer for an algorithm, displaying one question at a time on the screen, and moving to the next appropriate question or outcome according to whether Y or N is pressed on the keyboard.

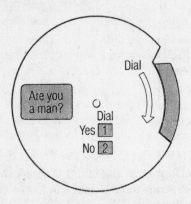

So far we have looked at algorithms for fault-finding machinery and for decision making. What else can they be used for? Anyone who has been known to write algorithms is often asked if he can write an algorithm for choosing a husband or wife, for deciding to which school to send his children, or for selecting which package holiday would be most suitable. If the subject is not based on logical decision making, for example how to choose a spouse in the United Kingdom, then the answer is a definite 'NO'. It might be quite possible in a country such as India, where marriages are arranged within an accepted code and are probably just as successful.

Certainly algorithms cannot be used to teach anyone anything. Their function is to enable people to carry out certain tasks and arrive at certain decisions. That is why they have been used in subjects such as those we have already seen. There is a body of opinion that holds it is immoral to do something without knowing why it is being done. This argument is often voiced against the production of fault-finding algorithms. Can this stance be genuinely maintained when there is so much information to be absorbed? Do these people know exactly what is happening when a button labelled '7' in a lift is pressed, the doors close and the lift goes up to the seventh floor, stops, and the doors open? Algorithms can be extremely useful to very busy people who cannot afford to make a mistake.

Those people in industry who have to operate within a legal framework, particularly those in personnel departments, have to make sure that they have 'got it right'. If an employee needs disciplining, what is the correct procedure? There is an algorithm on disciplinary procedure printed in Chapter 7.

Not only is there so much legislation that one must not fall foul of, there are also agreements with trade unions. The algorithm on shiftwork payment already quoted was produced to make sure that there was no infringement of such agreements.

As algorithms can be so useful and save so much time, why are they not used more extensively? One reason is that they are extremely difficult to write. Another is that people feel themselves threatened. A series of algorithms was produced for finding and correcting faults in the looms in a cotton weaving mill. Previously the foreman, or tackler, would deal with faults as they arose, and the weavers who were on piecework rates would have to wait until it was their turn to receive attention. Sometimes it took a long time to find and put right a fault, and waiting was obviously not popular. The method of training the tacklers was for them to work with a skilled man and 'learn by experience' – to sit by Nellie. While the algorithms were in process of being produced, it soon became evident that some faults occurred much more frequently than others, and this was allowed for in the production of the algorithms. When the job was finished and a small book of twenty flow-charts was printed, one of the old tacklers, who had been most helpful in its production, held it up and said, 'There's my twenty years' experience.'

That was a long time ago, and no doubt however many cotton weaving looms remain are now computer operated – but none the less the attitude remains; if there is a mystique surrounding a job, whoever does that job is resistant to change. Unfortunately, job mystique seems often to be inversely related to the knowledge and skill required for the job. In fact, many jobs which involve making decisions based on a fixed set of logical considerations could well be left to less able people supplied with algorithms, while the experts are left free for more difficult and important work.

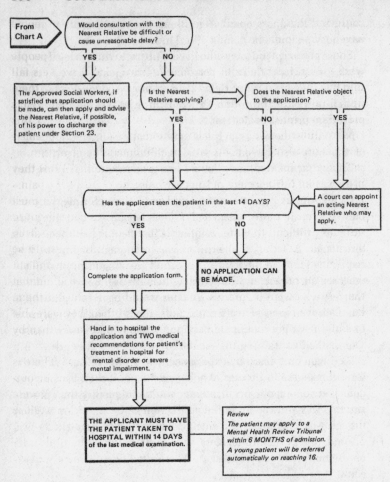

From Chart A

Would consultation with the Nearest Relative be difficult or cause unreasonable delay?

YES — The Approved Social Workers, if satisfied that application should be made, can then apply and advise the Nearest Relative, if possible, of his power to discharge the patient under Section 23.

NO — Is the Nearest Relative applying?

Does the Nearest Relative object to the application?

YES

NO

YES — A court can appoint an acting Nearest Relative who may apply.

Has the applicant seen the patient in the last 14 DAYS?

YES — Complete the application form.

NO — NO APPLICATION CAN BE MADE.

Hand in to hospital the application and TWO medical recommendations for patient's treatment in hospital for mental disorder or severe mental impairment.

THE APPLICANT MUST HAVE THE PATIENT TAKEN TO HOSPITAL WITHIN 14 DAYS of the last medical examination.

Review
The patient may apply to a Mental Health Review Tribunal within 6 MONTHS of admission.
A young patient will be referred automatically on reaching 16.

There are those who object to the use of algorithms because they 'deskill' jobs; this is the habitual cry of the machine-breakers and the computer smashers. After all, there is nothing to stop people from finding out a great deal about their jobs, while using algorithms to make sure that they get things right in the learning time. It is interesting that with the algorithms used for water treatment, described earlier in this chapter, a self-instruction text on water chemistry was produced, so that those who wanted to know why could find out. Not everyone wants to know, and a lot of people haven't time to find out.

Some of those who genuinely haven't time to find out are people whose job involves a great deal of legislation. Social workers fall into this category, and algorithms have been provided to help them find their way through what they called the legal maze. When Acts of Parliament are updated, as the Mental Health Act was in 1983, this creates confusion. On page 130 is a section of the algorithm for emergency admissions which was written after the updating.

The writers of algorithms have a heavy responsibility. What they produce must be believed in. Not only must the algorithm be painstakingly constructed, it must be checked by the expert, and it must be tried out by potential users. An experiment was carried out to discover whether people – mostly middle-aged to elderly – who would be affected by the Leasehold Reform Act of 1967 would be happy using both flow-chart and list-structure algorithms to find out whether they could acquire or extend their leases. It was found that they were unhappy if the algorithms were simply presented to them, but if a few minutes were spent in guiding them, then they were able to sort out their situations much more quickly and easily than by using the Ministry of Housing's leaflet.

There are conventions in the presentation of algorithms. There is for example really no need for the questions, instructions or outcomes in flow-charts to be enclosed (and in the early ones they were not, as the water treatment algorithm shows) but some writers use different-shaped boxes for different things:

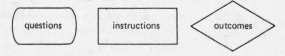

and some thicken the lines for outcome boxes:

The 'YES' and 'NO' should always be close to the box to make it easy to follow the right line.

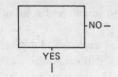

Whether there should be arrows or just lines is debatable. The only reason for arrows is that they confirm that the correct path has been taken:

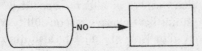

The format of the algorithm must be dictated by the logic of the questions. It cannot be squeezed to fit neatly into a page. Often, after the algorithm is constructed, it can be tidied up without damage; boxes can often be repositioned to avoid lines crossing over.

Let us take a very easy example:

> The entrance fee to a stately home is £2
> unless you are under 18 when it is £1,
> but if you are a member of the Historic Homes
> Trust* it is half the ordinary price.

There are two conditions:

over/under 18

member/non-member of HHT

We will start with membership:

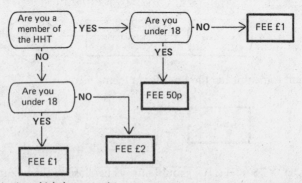

* an organization which does not exist

Rearranged, it becomes:

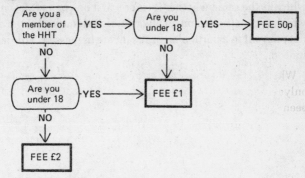

By rearranging YES and NO answers, one box has been saved and the algorithm looks tidier.

Sometimes an illustration is worth a great many words, and algorithms can be constructed using pictures. This is an extract from a picture-algorithm to enable fruit growers to diagnose diseases of apple trees:

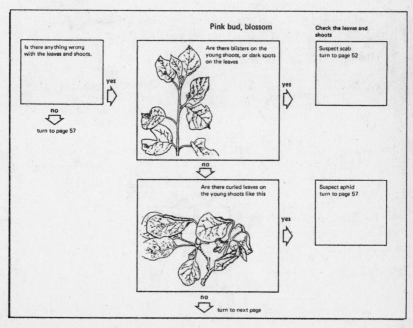

In Chapter 15 we discuss the form used for obtaining a passport, which is the same whether it is for a first one or a replacement, and which is constructed on an algorithmic principle. All the questions not relevant to a particular applicant are by-passed. This is progress indeed.

12 It Won't Work

The need for communication in user manuals

As has already been said, in the home, the office and the factory we are surrounded by equipment. Not much nowadays is mechanical; most of it is electrical or electronic. It will do such a lot for us – if only we can manage to use it, and use it to its full potential, keep it functioning, and cope with its minor hiccups. Unfortunately the people who invent, design and make all this equipment often seem unable to communicate with the end users. We all know how galling it is to buy a new widget extractor, get it home, carry out what we *think* the instruction book is telling us, plug it in, switch it on . . . and nothing happens! However diligently we read and reread the instruction book, we can't understand how to get it going. We telephone the salesman, and often, as he is unable to offer much help at a distance, another visit is required. Manufacturers and agents rarely cost the time involved in dealing with problems which the customer should be able to solve but can't because the instructions are inadequate.

It is worth while for manufacturers to have user manuals written and designed by experts in communication, rather than by experts in the subject. Not only will it save a deal of aggravation, but it should help to sell the product. Buyers are becoming more good-instructions aware. The most important thing is that user literature should be considered as an integral part of the product, not as something someone knocks up at the last minute. The designer should have the user in the back of his mind all the time. However elegant the product may be, without knobs or other protuberances, there is no excuse for putting the 'on' switch of an electric typewriter where not only is it invisible, but it is in a place where no one would dream of looking for it.

Mechanical devices had one great advantage: it was usually possible to see how they worked; and the corollary was that when they
didn't, the cause of the malfunction could often also be seen. If
pushing the pedals failed to make your bicycle go along, you could
see at a glance that the chain had come off, and you could put it on
again. Not much could go wrong with a wringer; but if your tumble
dryer stops tumbling, you have a problem. You take out the instruction book; there is probably no section on Minor Faults You Can Put
Right Yourself, so you send for the repair man. In the old days of
wireless sets with valves, if one didn't light up, you knew it had to
be replaced. Not so with transistors.

Not only can we not see how equipment works nowadays, but it is
often multi-functional. The old-fashioned gramophone only played
records; it did not silently record music being broadcast from the
Albert Hall a couple of hundred miles away, and do all the other
things a so-called music centre does today.

We should be able to make the best use of all that our advanced
technology offers us; so those who design and make must tell those
who use how to achieve this, and what to do when something goes
wrong. Users must know what they can put right themselves, and
what must be left to the expert.

Any piece of equipment, be it a typewriter, a mainframe computer
or a jumbo jet aeroplane, needs user instructions. One fault in a great
number of instruction leaflets and manuals is that they tell you how
the thing works, instead of how to start it and keep it functioning,
how to make it do all the things which it is designed to do, and how
to fault-find it. Much equipment is only half used because of lack of
instructions: large computers are used as desk calculators; sophisticated computerized telephone systems are used in the same way as
ordinary house phones.

One difficulty which seems to be commonly experienced by the
writers of instructions is that of assessing the users. The manuals
supplied with cars provide an interesting example of this. First, one
is told which is the clutch pedal and that it must be depressed before
the gear lever is moved; later, there comes a deal of information
about torque; and last comes that wonderful wiring diagram which
makes finding one's way through the Hampton Court maze seem like
child's play. It is hard to imagine any car owner wanting to learn

how to change gear by reading the manual; or bothering about torque after he'd bought the car; or using the wiring diagram. Who are these manuals written for?

The booklet supplied with a washing machine starts, reasonably enough, with instructions for installing it. However, it omits to say that only a qualified plumber could carry this out. Unfortunately the amateur would discover this only after he had dismantled the house water-supply system and reached the point of no return. He should preferably be directed to read through all the installation instructions before beginning, to make sure that he can do the whole job, has the tools to do it and, if it is beyond his capabilities, get professional help.

In Chapter 3 we showed this extract from a typewriter manual. You were asked to make a list of things which make it difficult to follow the instructions.

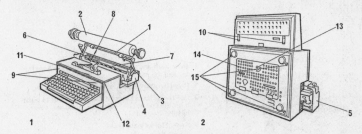

REMOVAL OF COVERS
The side covers are retained by the attachment springs on either side of the machine, which may be accessed by lifting the paper bail (1-1). The platen (1-2) is held by the retaining levers (1-3) which must be raised to extract the platen. The cover (1-4) and the paper table assembly (1-7) are removed by loosening the cover screws (2-5) and disconnecting them from the attachment clips (1-8). Before this can be done, it is necessary to remove the paper trough (1-6). The keyboard cover, secured by two hexagonal bolts (1-9) and captive clips (2-10) is removed to allow the keyboard to be cleared. The typebar cover (1-11) held in situ by hinge springs and screws (1-12) is then lifted off. Turning a captive screw (2-13) loosens the inspection cover (2-14) and removing the four base plate screws (2-15) allows the chassis to be cleared, thus completing the dismantling procedure.

A. The diagrams:
    (1) As the numbers attached to the leader lines go from 1 to 15, there is no point in labelling the diagrams 1 and 2.
    (2) The leader line 2–5 does not go to screws at all.

B. The instructions:

(1) There is a mixture of description, explanation and instruction.

(2) Unfamiliar words like 'accessed' are used.

(3) Technical terms are used which cannot be understood by looking at the diagrams.

(4) There is a mistake: only one screw needs to be removed.

(5) Half-way through comes 'Before this can be done . . .' It is a very old joke that at the end of instructions on how to take apart a piece of electrical equipment comes, 'Before starting, disconnect from the electricity supply', but this shows that it can be true.

This is an extract from a genuine manual. The version of the instructions below was written by the person who removed the wrong screw 2–5, and was hit by the paper bail as it flew off. The note to 8 warns against doing this. Foreseeing likely mistakes is helpful.

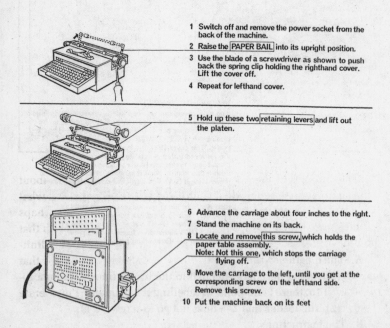

1 Switch off and remove the power socket from the back of the machine.

2 Raise the PAPER BAIL into its upright position.

3 Use the blade of a screwdriver as shown to push back the spring clip holding the righthand cover. Lift the cover off.

4 Repeat for lefthand cover.

5 Hold up these two retaining levers and lift out the platen.

6 Advance the carriage about four inches to the right.

7 Stand the machine on its back.

8 Locate and remove this screw, which holds the paper table assembly.
Note: Not this one, which stops the carriage flying off.

9 Move the carriage to the left, until you get at the corresponding screw on the lefthand side. Remove this screw.

10 Put the machine back on its feet

This is the first instruction in the manual which is supposed to tell one how to operate a television set:

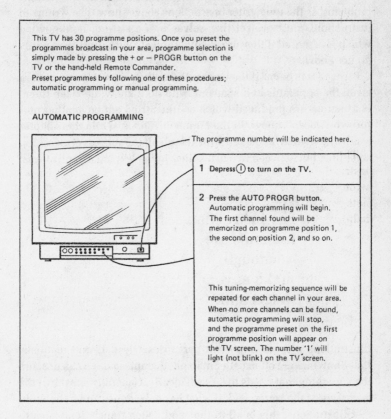

This TV has 30 programme positions. Once you preset the programmes broadcast in your area, programme selection is simply made by pressing the + or − PROGR button on the TV or the hand-held Remote Commander.

Preset programmes by following one of these procedures; automatic programming or manual programming.

AUTOMATIC PROGRAMMING

The programme number will be indicated here.

1 Depress Ⓘ to turn on the TV.

2 Press the AUTO PROGR button. Automatic programming will begin. The first channel found will be memorized on programme position 1, the second on position 2, and so on.

This tuning-memorizing sequence will be repeated for each channel in your area.

When no more channels can be found, automatic programming will stop, and the programme preset on the first programme position will appear on the TV screen. The number '1' will light (not blink) on the TV screen.

The supplier of the set, who is extremely knowledgeable about the equipment he sells, when confronted with this and asked what it meant, said, after a long look at the page, 'I don't know . . . perhaps it means that it does it itself . . . perhaps it means if you press that button, and then . . . I should have to play with it . . .' He then admitted that so many of the user instructions supplied are useless that he and his colleagues have to use their knowledge and experience – and waste a good deal of their time – in finding out how to operate the equipment he sells.

Writing instructions to do anything in the slightest bit complicated is not easy. Even getting things in the right order presents problems, as the typewriter instructions above show. The writers of instructions must project themselves into a state of not-knowing which is essential if they are to communicate with users who really do not know.

Perhaps it is better if the writers themselves do not know, but are given the apparatus and someone who does know; between them, instructions are produced which are then tried out on another person who doesn't know. In the *Financial Times*, while this chapter was being written, appeared an article about the success of a desktop computer, but between two black lines in the text in large print was:

**'The instruction
manuals are
enough
to make anyone's
heart sink'**

Illustrations play an important part in user leaflets and manuals. Line-drawings are often better than photographs, which can obscure the very thing that needs to be seen clearly. Generally speaking, the fewer words the better; and, if what has to be done can be shown in the illustrations, this is all to the good. Often translations have to be made into several languages, and the fewer words there are to translate, the fewer mistakes, ambiguities and difficulties there are likely to be.

Opposite is an admirable page from a teaching manual for engineering craft apprentices. The drawings are clear, and the text is minimal:

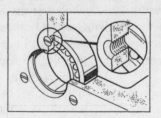

Bearing removal screws

Some housings have tapped and countersunk holes behind the bearing. These holes are normally fitted with short screws to prevent the threads becoming blocked with dirt.

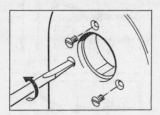

To remove the bearing:

(a) Remove the screws from the holes.

(b) Select the same number of screws that will fit the holes and are long enough to remove the bearing.

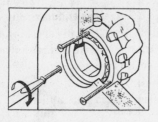

(c) Fit the longer screws and tighten them equally by small amounts to remove the bearing slowly from its housing. Take care to keep the bearing square to its housing.

In some circumstances, symbols can be used instead of drawings or photographs. It is perfectly obvious what the symbols mean in this instruction book on how to use a key phone with special facilities.

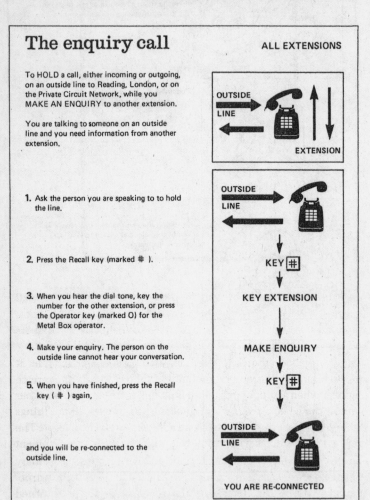

The enquiry call

ALL EXTENSIONS

To HOLD a call, either incoming or outgoing, on an outside line to Reading, London, or on the Private Circuit Network, while you MAKE AN ENQUIRY to another extension.

You are talking to someone on an outside line and you need information from another extension.

OUTSIDE LINE

EXTENSION

1. Ask the person you are speaking to to hold the line.

OUTSIDE LINE

2. Press the Recall key (marked #).

KEY #

3. When you hear the dial tone, key the number for the other extension, or press the Operator key (marked O) for the Metal Box operator.

KEY EXTENSION

4. Make your enquiry. The person on the outside line cannot hear your conversation.

MAKE ENQUIRY

5. When you have finished, press the Recall key (#) again,

KEY #

and you will be re-connected to the outside line.

OUTSIDE LINE

YOU ARE RE-CONNECTED

On the other hand, symbols can be very difficult to 'translate'. Any driver could be forgiven for failing to take in this one:

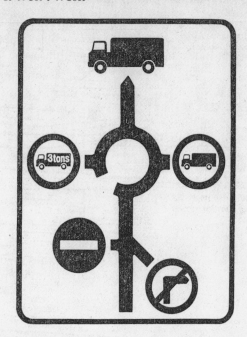

Illustrations of whatever kind should be integrated with the text. The necessity of turning over the page to refer to a diagram or photograph is very off-putting, particularly if it is covered with numbers and leader-lines.

However good equipment may be, there comes a time when it stops working. It wastes a lot of time and money to call in a service engineer when a minor adjustment is all that is needed. On the other hand, it can be disastrous when someone sets to work to put things right with a great deal of enthusiasm and very little knowledge. The more common faults likely to develop in any piece of equipment can easily be determined; they can be divided into those the ordinary user can put right and those which must be left to the expert. Instructions can then be provided for the first category, and the user warned off tackling the second.

Manuals which tell the user how the thing works, instead of how to operate it, have already been referred to. These usually assume that, if the equipment malfunctions, the operator can then work

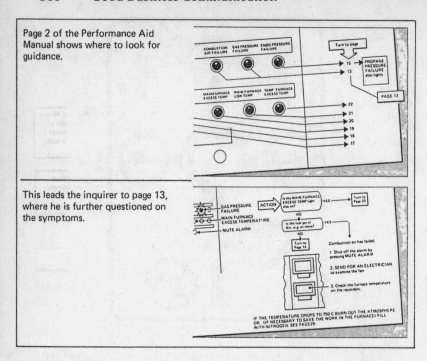

Page 2 of the Performance Aid Manual shows where to look for guidance.

This leads the inquirer to page 13, where he is further questioned on the symptoms.

out why and put things right. Sometimes this is neither easy nor practical. A very large continuous furnace used for tempering metal components was provided with just such a manual. Occasionally explosive gases could build up in the furnace – in which case an alarm sounded and lights flashed on a panel. If the fault was not corrected within twenty minutes, a major explosion could occur, and certainly the work load would be ruined. Time spent on the regular training, which would have been necessary if workers on all three shifts were to be able to deal with an emergency which might never occur, was wasteful. The manual was useless. The company owning the furnace had a special guide produced. This started with a diagram of the lights panel. If an alarm sounded, the user looked to see which light was showing, found this on the diagram and followed the appropriate instructions.

An extremely effective tool for fault-finding is the algorithm, as we saw in the last chapter. These algorithms are usually produced

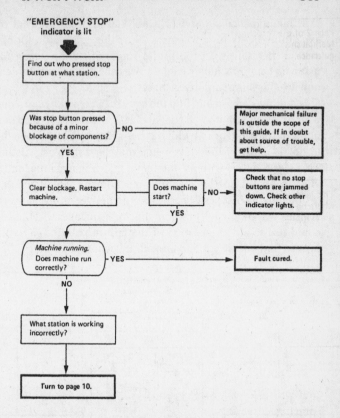

"EMERGENCY STOP" indicator is lit

Find out who pressed stop button at what station.

Was stop button pressed because of a minor blockage of components? —NO→ Major mechanical failure is outside the scope of this guide. If in doubt about source of trouble, get help.

YES

Clear blockage. Restart machine. → Does machine start? —NO→ Check that no stop buttons are jammed down. Check other indicator lights.

YES

Machine running. Does machine run correctly? —YES→ Fault cured.

NO

What station is working incorrectly?

Turn to page 10.

in flow-chart form, and the user simply follows a path through the algorithm by answering YES/NO questions. The example given above is from a series produced for diagnosing faults in an assembly line. Before these algorithms were produced, when something went wrong the operator had to decide whether to call the engineer or to try to put it right himself. When a fault happens now, the operator follows the path through the algorithm until he finds the source of the trouble. He is then told what to do or, if the remedy is beyond his competence, he is told to call in the expert. The production manager reported that these algorithms had reduced training time for maintenance staff by between one and three months; and when a fitter is used to the book, he can diagnose a fault in seconds. The company was able to reduce the number of maintenance staff from 22 to 17; labour turnover in the department also dropped. The nightshift maintenance supervisor said: 'I used to spend a lot of time explaining faults to newcomers. Now they pick up a lot of information themselves. In the initial stages of training someone, the manuals have probably saved 25 per cent of my time, which I can now use for more important things.'

Sometimes, in order to find the cause of a breakdown in a machine which has an automatic sequence, it is necessary to recognize the point in the sequence at which it has stopped. This can be difficult to do, as many of the movements may be difficult to distinguish. This was the case with an automatic grinding machine, and it was vital to avoid lengthy machine breakdowns which would have resulted in the company being late with deliveries of a new product. A guide was produced, first showing the sequences that the machine could use to aid recognition of the failure point, then explaining how to find out why it had broken down at that point.

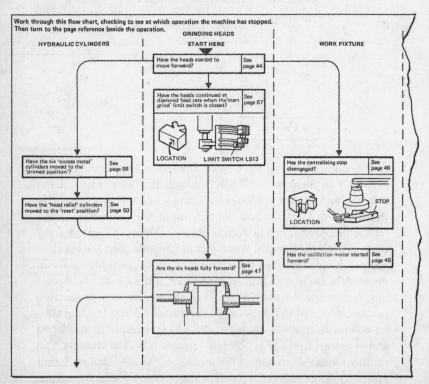

Sometimes it is necessary to train operators without conventional instruction which would be impractical. This was the case with new filtration plants for effluent treatment, because there were a large number of operators, geographically scattered. A manual was designed in which the illustrations and text were combined into an effective training and performance aid. The words, as it were, 'mechanize' the illustration instead of merely annotating it.

An extract from the original operations manual:

(19) Screw up the clamping nuts on the tiebars until the number of threads exposed between the cylinder ends and the locknuts have been reduced to four. Switch on the hydraulic pump units, close the by-pass valves and bring the hydraulic jacks up to pressure. Spin up the locknuts until they are hand tight against the cylinder ends, release each locknut by one quarter of a turn, open the drain valves on the hydraulic power units and switch off the units.

(20) Extend the filtrate collection trays under the press, close the drain valve and open the feed valve leaving the press ready for the next filtration cycle.

An extract from the new operations manual:

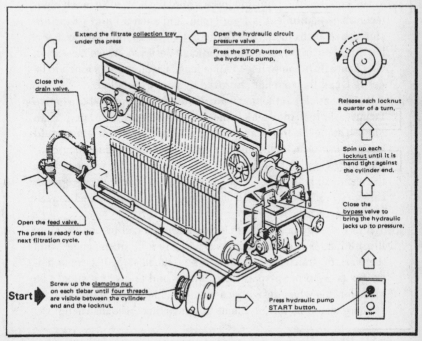

The little tourist shops in Dubrovnik have notices on their doors which announce:

> # Non-stop
> ## 9.00 - 21.00

– which certainly create an impression of the assistants' ceaseless activity for twelve-hour stretches. Like so many mistranslations, it is funny; and, like examples of gobbledegook, collections are now being made of these 'funnies'. However, if the translation is of a users' instruction manual, the jokes soon wear thin. 'Non-stop' for 'open' could cause confusion in some circumstances. So much high-technology equipment is from Japan, and such a lot of precision-engineered instruments are German, that translation is necessary, but this is not often given the attention it deserves. As we have seen, user manuals in the writer's native language often leave much to be desired, and they are not improved by poor translation.

It is essential that the translator should be someone whose native language is that into which the instructions are translated. If an English manual is to be translated into German, the translator should be German, not an English person with a degree in modern languages including German. He may know Goethe well but will not have the technical knowledge or language to write about microscopes or cameras. Preferably, the translator should know the subject as well as the language.

It has already been said that the more that can be conveyed by illustration, the less dependence will there be on language, and therefore on translation. It should be remembered that some languages take up more space than others, and allowance should be made for this when designing a manual which is to be translated.

There would be few problems in translating these instructions:

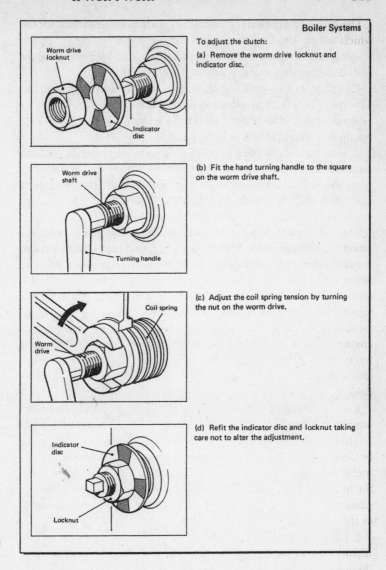

Boiler Systems

To adjust the clutch:

(a) Remove the worm drive locknut and indicator disc.

Worm drive locknut

Indicator disc

(b) Fit the hand turning handle to the square on the worm drive shaft.

Worm drive shaft

Turning handle

(c) Adjust the coil spring tension by turning the nut on the worm drive.

Coil spring

Worm drive

(d) Refit the indicator disc and locknut taking care not to alter the adjustment.

Indicator disc

Locknut

One confusion which upsets translations is the belief that American and English are the same language. They are not, and the differences are more fundamental than calling a biscuit a cookie, and the pavement a sidewalk. If instructions are to be produced for the American market, they should be rewritten by an American. Unfortunately a lot of Japanese manuals are translated by Americans for both the American and English markets.

Companies exist which specialize in technical translations, but care must be taken in selecting one of them. The result of their labours should always be tried out on a sample of the people for whom it is intended before being printed.

A great number of people complain about user manuals, for both domestic and factory equipment, and have been doing so for a long time. As technology becomes 'higher' and 'higher', the problem of operation and fault-finding increases. Perhaps only when buyers consider the instructions to be an important part of the total 'package' and refuse to buy if the instructions are inadequate will the situation be improved. Writing user instructions is difficult, but there are some individuals and two or three companies able to do this.

13 *See and Hear*

Audio-visual communication

Almost anyone who writes about audio-visual aids points out that we remember only 20 per cent of what we hear, 30 per cent of what we see, and 50 per cent of what we both hear and see. These figures need to be taken with more than a pinch of salt, because we can hear, or see, or hear and see, with little, some, a lot, or maximum attention. The degree of attention depends on motivation. You will glue your eyes to the television news if you think that you may see yourself. You will listen with bated breath to hear the end of a thriller on the radio. If you want to get on in your job and there are audio-visual aids to help you, you will listen and watch, unless the slide-tape or film is so bad or so boring that even your motivation cannot keep your attention alive. So it would be better just to say that, other things being equal, we remember a little of what we hear, more of what we see, and most of what we hear and see. This is a good reason for using audio-visual aids.

By definition, a visual aid is something which can be seen, and is a help to someone making a presentation of some kind. Probably the visual aid first encountered by most people was in the classroom, when they were part of the audience and a teacher was making the presentation. For the not-so-young it was the blackboard, for the rest, probably the white or yellow board. Now it is called the chalk-board. If they sat near the back of the class no doubt they, at some time, said, 'Please, Miss, I can't see the board,' which meant that they couldn't see what the teacher had written on it. This illustrates the point that, to live up to its name, a visual aid must be seen by the whole audience.

A board (or its paper counterpart, the flip chart) still has some definite advantages over most sophisticated visual aids. It is cheap, generally available, and needs little preparation. A board quickly gets filled up and has to be erased, whereas a flip chart has many pages and can be kept, and some pages can be prepared in advance. Boards and flip charts have the disadvantage that, in order to write on them, the speaker must turn his back to the audience. If he goes on talking, he will not be heard so well. Writing on a board or large sheet of paper is not as easy as it seems; practice is absolutely essential. The writer must also find out how large his writing must be for the person farthest away to be able to read what he has written. Obviously neither boards nor flip charts are suitable for large audiences, nor for writing or drawing something elaborate, as too long will be spent turned away from the audience. Probably their best use is for writing unusual words, brief summaries, or numbers or equations which are difficult to take in when they are only heard.

There are a number of different kinds of boards on sale. If they are made of coated steel, they can be used for magnetic displays as well as for writing on. Some are also suitable for use as projection screens.

After the board, the next visual aid we encountered in the classroom was probably a map or a picture. Again, there were problems in seeing details, unless one was in one of the front rows. If these aids are used, it must be checked that what is meant to be seen, can be seen. This may seem obvious, but presenters often forget to check whether writing or details can be seen at a distance.

The episcope, or opaque projector, seems to have gone out of fashion, but it is extremely useful and is still to be found in manufacturers' catalogues. It projects enlarged images in the original colours. Ordinary books, charts, pictures, maps can be used, so there is no need to make transparencies or slides. If it can also be used to project slides, the instrument is called an epidiascope. It is however necessary to darken the room to use an episcope and this can be a drawback.

One of the most useful pieces of visual equipment is the overhead projector. This can be used in a lighted room and is simple to operate. Transparencies, or film for writing on, are put on the glass working surface. Perhaps the greatest advantage of using an overhead projector is that the speaker is always facing his audience. He can point to anything he wants to draw attention to on the transparency without having to turn round to the screen. He must be careful not to stand in such a position that he covers part of what is being projected on the screen. He can write on transparent foil with special pens which are made with various coloured inks. The projector must be switched off when not actually being used.

Overhead projectors tend to reproduce the image on the screen with a keystone distortion: instead of being rectangular, it is shaped like the stone at the top of an arch. Tilting the screen slightly can cure this.

10 × 10 transparencies can be made on the office copying machine from existing printed material, and do-it-yourself kits can be bought with which professional-looking visuals can be made. Bright colours can be used, which liven up a talk. A transparency should not be cluttered, and as little text as possible should be included. Transparencies can be masked with tracing paper which can be peeled off bit by bit to reveal what is underneath. The reverse can also be done: up to four overlays can be put on the transparency, but more than four take away from the brightness of the image. Some presenters use two projectors, one with film to write on and one to show ready-made transparencies.

Slides are probably the most favoured visual aids; they are usually made on 35mm colour reversal film, and mounted in 2″ × 2″ glass mounts. These protect the slides, make them easy to clean and prevent them going out of focus because of the heat generated when they are projected. Anyone proficient with a camera can make 35mm slides, but for important presentations a professional photographer should be employed. Slides are difficult to handle, and it should be borne in mind that glass mounts break if they are dropped! It is all too easy to project them upside down, sideways, and back to front, which makes seven wrong ways, and although this may be amusing at first, it soon becomes irritating and appears amateurish. One way of making sure that the slides are loaded correctly is to mark each one so that the viewing side and top can easily be seen.

There are an enormous number of slide projectors. For presentations, an automatic projector with a straight or circular slide tray is necessary. Modern projectors produce a very high-quality image, but blacking-out the room is necessary. When the slide tray is loaded, the slides will appear in the order in which they are put in the tray. There are random access projectors which will project any slide selected, but there is a delay of about three seconds before a selected slide appears.

A 35mm or 16mm film can be used as a strip, but is obviously less versatile than slides, as the images will always be projected in the same order. It is cheaper than slides, particularly if many copies are needed. The light needs to be dimmed to show film strips. Slides and film strips can be bought ready-made, and they are usually of a high quality. But, like all ready-mades, they seldom fit the needs of the presenter or the audience perfectly.

Although we frequently talk of visual aids, 'audio aids' is an unfamiliar phrase. However, recorded sound can be extremely helpful in a talk or presentation. Describing a sound is very difficult indeed: the difference between the sound of a machine running sweetly and not, needs to be heard to be appreciated. A sound recording of the Chairman's remarks before presenting the annual report to employees might be better than a printed version of it. Certainly, in the preparation of a presentation, a tape-recorder is essential both for timing and for hearing what you sound like. It is easy to send tapes by post, and a recorded message can be more effective than a letter, as all the emphases and inflexions are there. Today, people are used to high-fidelity recording, and they expect this standard in a presentation. In a room of any size with a large audience, the furnishings and the people absorb the frequencies that make words audible. Just as visual aids need to be seen, so audio aids need to be heard. Suitable loudspeakers must be used, and they must be placed above the heads of the audience. If they are on the floor, the people at the front will be deafened, and those at the back won't hear.

So, if we put visual aids and recorded sound together, we have audio-visual aids. Technology has made the whole subject intimidating, there is so much to choose from.

Audio-visual aids in business can be used for training, informing and selling. It must be remembered that they are aids, they do not serve 'instead of', nor do they necessarily make the job easier. Using them properly does ensure that at least some preparation has been done. They help in preventing monotony, as they break up a presentation; and they can also keep the presenter from straying from his planned talking – although overhead projector transparencies can do this just as well.

What is there to choose from? There are slide-tape projectors which can be used in various ways of increasing complexity. There are movies of different kinds. There are video recorders, which can also be used to project slide-tapes and movies.

A single slide projector, synchronized with a tape-recorder linked to loudspeakers, is probably the simplest form of audio-visual hardware, and programmes for it are moderately easy, and moderately cheap, to make or have made. They do have one great drawback: it takes about a second for a projector to advance from one slide to the next, so there is usually a gap between them, which is disconcerting. The sound is synchronized to the slide projection by having two tracks on the tape, one carrying the sound and the other controlling the slide changing. These slide-tape programmes are widely used and most effective, but are not suitable for important presentations, or for very large audiences.

The solution to the problem of the gap between the slides is to employ two or more projectors and a dissolve unit, which makes one image dissolve into the other. This is, in essence, a very old technique used in the magic lantern days by turning the gaslight down and performing some tricks of legerdemain with the slides.

For most people and situations, two projectors are enough. Two circular slide trays will hold 160 slides, which suffice for most presentations. To have to pause to change the trays spoils the continuity. However, three or more projectors can be used to show more slides and get more effects. With three projectors, more equipment is needed, including a 'memory dissolve' unit, and it all becomes more complicated.

More than three projectors can be used – up to 120 have been known – but if more than three are used, more than one screen is necessary. More elaborate effects can be obtained, as higher speeds are possible. These multivision (English) or multi image (American) programmes are not for ordinary business use, but only for very up-market presentations.

If a high-quality production, including movement, is needed, to be seen by large audiences, a movie is best. Sound film has become the pinnacle of audio-visual achievement. While its possibilities are almost endless, it does have its limitations for business use: once made it cannot be altered, brought up to date for example. To see a movie which shows many cars, but none with a registration letter later than Y, dates its production to not later than 31 July 1983, which may or may not matter. An out-of-date slide can simply be replaced.

The need for movement must be stressed, as movies are many times more expensive than slide-tape productions; to make a film where one man talks and points to various photographs, and the only movement happens when he walks from one to another, is extremely wasteful. Equally so is a movie about arthritis with many still photographs of joints in various conditions and only one short sequence showing a person walking. Movies can be made by photographing real people in real or simulated situations. They can also be made by photographing a very great number of drawings, each successive drawing showing a very slight change of position, so when they are shown at speed the effect of movement is given. This is called animation and is the most expensive way of making movies, as the number of drawings necessary is enormous. This technique is used a lot in making commercials for showing on independent television channels. Most people are familiar with the Walt Disney movies which used this technique. There is also a snob value about films, which sometimes leads companies to commission them when a less expensive slide-tape programme would serve the same purpose. It must also be remembered that movies can be shown on a larger screen than slide-tapes.

For business purposes, a 16mm film is most widely used. It is claimed that 16mm film projectors can be found anywhere in the world where audio-visual programmes are known, so it is obviously a very good medium if your movie is to be widely distributed. There are lightweight compact portable projectors available which are self-threading and so no more difficult to use than a cassette tape-recorder. Movies must be projected in a darkened room, and a screen up to four metres wide can be used.

The standard for films such as are shown in an entertainment cinema is 35mm. These will rarely be needed for business purposes, unless a movie is to be made for some very special purpose and will be shown to large audiences. These movies will not be shown by an amateur, and a professional projectionist is required.

The great majority of 16mm and 35mm films carry the sound track on the edge of the film. It is recorded separately and dubbed on to the film in the last stage of production. It is possible to change the sound track on an existing film or to have extra tracks.

Most people are familiar with television sets, even if they don't possess one. Also, many people who have a television set have a video recorder as well. Television sets are made for the average room in an average house and, except in the bars of public houses, not for public viewing. This is a limitation that the users of video cassettes for presentations must recognize. Large screens can be obtained, but the quality of the picture is not as good as that on domestic receivers.

Half-inch video tape is presented in a cassette. Unlike audio cassettes which are all standard, there are four different types of cassette, three of them widely used. Unfortunately, recorders and cassettes are not interchangeable. The three in common use are VCR (Video Cassette Recorder), which is used a great deal on the Continent; VHS (Video Home System), which has the biggest share of the domestic market worldwide; and Betamax, which is next to VHS in popularity. The fourth is Eumantic, which uses a 3/4" video tape; it was originally developed for industrial use and now produces video tapes of the highest quality. It is possible to convert from one standard to another, but this is very expensive. If video cassettes are being made for presentations when another company's equipment is to be used, it is better if two versions are produced, VHS and Betamax. This is simpler than carrying the recorder and television set around. The television often used with a video recorder for presentations is called a monitor. An ordinary television set can be used and is called a receiver monitor, as it can also receive broadcast programmes.

It is possible for a programme to be transferred from one medium to another. A slide-tape presentation using two projectors will be cumbersome to carry about, involving the recorder and the loudspeakers, as well as the projectors; if the trays loaded with slides are not going to spill, some device such as putting sellotape round the outside must be used. If this programme is transferred to video cassette, the presenter will have one small box to carry, as no doubt there will be a television set and video recorder where the visit is being made. Remember: find out whether it is a VHS or Betamax system, before the visit is made.

Transfer of movie to video is often made, again usually for convenience. These transfers can be made only by specialist companies, as expensive and sophisticated equipment is required.

Computers are being used increasingly in the audio-visual world. Complicated slides can be made using computer-generated graphics; these are not restricted to charts and graphs but can include pictures. These slides can be as good as those produced photographically, but they can be expensive if high quality is wanted. There are companies specializing in this field.

Animated moving pictures can also be produced by computer. These are used, for example, to introduce broadcast television programmes. They are a very effective gimmick but are extremely expensive to produce.

Self-instruction using a microcomputer instead of a text is interactive, as the learner carries on a conversation with the computer; but the term 'interactive program' is usually taken to mean a combination of audio-visual and computer technologies. This is a most interesting development and would augur well for a revival of interest in programmed instruction, if only the technique of writing the software had developed along with the development of the hardware, but unfortunately this has not been the case.

So far we have considered the hardware and what kind of software is to be used with it. These conventional terms are very misleading. 'Hardware', the equipment used, makes sense. 'Software', meaning the audio-visual programmes, does not. Slides, cassettes, transparencies, and disks are just as 'hard' to the touch as equipment. Only the preliminary stage, the writing on paper, is soft. It seems a pity that the use of computer terminology has spread so widely.

Apart from its entertainment value, however splendid a movie or slide-tape is, it is the content of the programme which matters. Spectacular photography often makes an audience forget what the programme was intended to convey. Those in a company who are responsible for buying off-the-shelf programmes or commissioning made-to-measure ones should make sure that they are buying a message not a medium. The difficulty of writing good training and self-instructional programmes is discussed in the relevant chapters. It cannot be stressed too much that equipment costing £100 or so, with an excellent but cheap slide-tape, will be more effective than a poor movie costing tens of thousands of pounds, shown on equally expensive equipment.

Audio-visual programmes, whether one-projector slide-tapes or full-length movies, are the result of several functions which must be carried out by at least four different people. Very important is the script writer. This is a highly professional job, and it is a great mistake to think that anyone can do it. The material has to be researched; it has to be written in language which sounds well; and the visuals have to be planned so that the illustrator and photographer, if both are needed, know what is expected of them. The illustrator and photographer must be professionals, able to work with the script writer and interpret his wishes. There must be a voice or voices, or even a whole company of actors. The voice-over, the technical term for the narrator in a slide-tape programme, must be a professional. Amateurs do not sound right and they take a great deal longer to record a script than a professional. A voice-over agency will send tapes of various voices so that the most suitable one can be chosen. Sometimes, if the script demands it, more than one voice is used for variety. Perhaps equally as important as the script writer is the producer. If a company of actors is being used, this is obviously a different job from producing a slide-tape with one voice-over.

Producing even a short slide-tape involves a great deal of work: knowing what it is all about, having an overall mental picture of the finished production, and being able to communicate with the rest of the team. All the same, people in communications and training departments of companies make very good audio-visual programmes. The important thing is knowing what can be done in-house, and what it is wise to buy in.

Although it is customary to talk about 'audio-visual' if even a single slide is shown, it is better to divide visual from audio-visual communication aids, as they have been discussed in this chapter, leaving out the purely audio.

Visual aids

        actual objects, e.g. what you are selling in a
        marketing programme

boards: chalk

    magnetic

flip charts

overhead projectors

film strips

slides

Audio-visual aids

slide-tapes: single projector

      two or three with dissolve

      multi image/multivision

movies: 16mm

    35mm

video: directly filmed

    transferred

The question is: how do you choose? The solution may be made simpler by financial considerations: you can only have what your company allows you to afford. But, other things being equal, it is better to consider your objectives. To use the actual object being talked about or promoted is better than a deal of indirect description, particularly in a sales presentation. If the object is a jumbo jet or a piece of earth-moving equipment this is impossible, unless you are giving the presentation on an airfield or a building site, but this produces other problems.

Exercise: You are the Personnel Director of a large retail company with a chain of stores in most major towns in England and Wales. A new system of job-evaluation and appraisal has been introduced, and the personnel managers in all the stores have to explain this to the employees. As this is a touchy situation, it is essential that the managers get the message right. What visual aid(s) would you commission to help them? Suggestions will be found at the end of this chapter.

	Size of audience	Cost	Flexibility
Visual			
Actual objects	Small/medium	Nil (already existing)	None
Models	Small/medium	Low to high	None
Chalkboards and flip charts	Small/medium	Very low	Good
Overhead projector + transparencies	Small/medium	Low to medium	Good
35mm slides + projector	Small/medium	Medium	Medium
Film strip + projector	Small/medium	Medium to high	None
Audio-visual			
Slide-tape Single projector	Medium	Medium	None
Slide-tape 2+ projectors	Medium	Progressively more expensive	None
Movies 16mm	Large	Very high	None
Movies 35mm	Very large	Very high	None
Video	Small	Very high	None
Transferred to video	Small	Original cost + medium to transfer	None

If you choose any audio-visual medium using a projector, the image must fall on to a surface. A wall, matt-painted white, can be used for all ordinary purposes, including 16mm, but not 35mm movies. If such a wall is not available, a screen must be used. Most screens are made of matt white plastic, pvc based. For presentations outside a special room, a portable screen is needed.

Carrying audio-visual equipment can be a problem. Most manufacturers sell portable versions of equipment. Although these are convenient, as they are made to fit into carrying cases, they are disproportionately expensive. One redoubtable lady, who travels hundreds of miles annually giving audio-visual presentations for a charitable organization, carries all her equipment, including an ordinary 16mm projector, on the back seat of her Mini.

It is necessary to decide whether to buy equipment or hire it. or to buy some and hire some. This will necessarily depend on how much it is going to be used. If you plan regular presentations using the same media, it is obviously cost-effective to buy it, and you soon get to know your own equipment.

A small company will probably need boards, flip charts, an over-head projector, a two-projector slide-tape system, and a video recorder and monitor. A large company will no doubt have a visual-aid centre, complete with projection room.

If you were the Personnel Director referred to on page 160, the following are some suggestions for visual aids. Cost is unlikely to be a major consideration as the message is so important, so it is worth considering whether a movie would be the best medium. This will depend entirely on whether your explanation involves a lot of move-ment or not. It might be worth thinking about animation, as this is likely to attract and hold attention more than using real-life people and situations. If the cost of this is considered too great, then a twin-projector slide-tape, using the same kind of visuals as in the animation movie, would be suitable. As many presentations will be given, putting the movie or slide-tape on to video cassettes would be a sensible procedure.

It is essential, if you are going to use audio-visual equipment, that either you are able to operate it with no fuss and bother, or you have an operator. Reference will be made to Murphy in Chapter 16, on presentations but, for now, just remember his law: 'If a thing can go wrong, it will.' This is particularly true of audio-visual equipment during an important presentation.

14 Could Do Better . . .

Communication in reports

For most of us, our first acquaintance with a report came when we took one home from school at the end of term. It was probably on a printed form, with spaces for standard information along the top: class, term and year, average age of class, age of pupil; and, down the side, names of subjects with spaces for remarks by subject teachers; with, at the bottom, a space for some general comments by the head or class teacher.

We may have had to fill in a car accident report form, which usually includes a request to draw a diagram of the accident, like the one on page 164.

Reports on printed forms have the advantage of determining what information has to be given, and limiting its amount. Some, however, tell you that you may use the back of the form or an additional sheet of paper if this is necessary to answer questions such as 'Give full details of the incident which led to the employee's dismissal', and 'Please state how the accident happened and draw a diagram showing the width of the road, position of the vehicles involved and the direction in which originally proceeding. Comment where appropriate on speed and weather conditions'. There may be an implication that you ought to get it all in the space provided. Forms will be considered in the next chapter.

A report usually conveys some specific information to a specific person or body of people who need to know for some particular reason. A report is sometimes, but not often, verbal, for example the policeman's report of an incident, given from the witness box and so often guyed in films and plays. Reports are usually written or printed. Sometimes the information is given to anyone who cares to read it, as reports in newspapers; after all, newspapermen are called 'reporters'. Often the report is made in answer to a request for infor-

Description of Accident

Please state how accident happened and draw a diagram showing the width of the road, position of the vehicles involved and the direction in which originally proceeding. Comment where appropriate on speed and weather conditions.

Blame (Put 'x' in appropriate box)

Self	
Other Party	
Both	

Signature
Driver . . . .
(where other than Insured)

Date . . . .

Signature
Insured . . . .
(If Company add Rubber Stamp or state position held

mation; sometimes it is made because someone wants to give information, for example to back up a request for, say, typewriters to be replaced by word processors in the company's general office. This request might be made in a letter or, more briefly, in a memorandum; but if a reasoned request is made, and facts and figures are supplied to justify the expenditure and training time, it would be considered to be a report.

All of which indicates that it is difficult to define 'report'. The *Shorter Oxford Dictionary* gives 'a formal statement of the results of an investigation, or of any matter on which definite information is required, made by some person or body instructed to do so'. There are various stages which must be gone through in producing such a document:

1. the terms of reference clearly defined
2. the method of collecting the data decided
3. the results written down
4. the results analysed
5. the conclusions decided
6. the supporting material selected
7. the report written.

The terms of reference

Defining the exact terms of reference is essential, or the whole report may be useless. It must be known who asked for the report and why. It is likely to be a person, or persons, in authority who will commission a report. It can be HM government; the main board of a company; a director of a company; or a society – although if a report can be financed, and the information required can be obtained, anyone can call for it to be produced. What are its objectives? It may be to collect and analyse data and to make recommendations. If may be just to collect and analyse the data for someone else to make the recommendations. It could be to investigate the effectiveness of a certain line of action. Whatever it is, there must be no doubts or ambiguities. The limitation can be financial: the report must cost no more than a certain amount to produce; there must be a financial limit to carrying out the recommendations. Relations with a trade union may also have a limiting effect. For example, if the objective is to establish whether changing the line-layout in a factory would lead to increased production, any rearrangement would almost certainly need trade union approval, and this would probably not be obtained if the rearrangement involved reducing the workforce.

Collecting the data

The method of collecting the data must be decided. Often this involves employing experts, and generally it is more effective to do so. If scientific research is needed, this cannot be carried out by amateurs; if market research is needed, the same is true. Collecting information inside one's own company gives opportunities for getting those from whom the information is collected interested in the report. This co-operation can be extremely valuable, particularly if those people are going to be involved in carrying out the report's recommendations.

Writing down the results

Writing up anything is laborious, rewriting even more so. Probably each person involved in writing up the data for a report will have his own method.

This recording must not be confused with writing the report, although its essentials are the same: accuracy, brevity and clarity. One of the difficulties in achieving accuracy is to maintain objectivity. It is easy, for example, to confuse the opinions of people consulted with facts. An office manager, when asked for reasons for a higher than average turnover of office staff, said that it was because the office equipment was out of date. He really believed this to be true, but he also wanted a high-technology office.

The rules for brevity and clarity are the same as for any written communication, but for recording data, note-form is acceptable as this will be changed when the report is written.

Space should be left between lines and in margins to make it easy to make alterations and put in additions. For the same reason it is better to write on only one side of the paper. Pages of the same size are easier to keep together than odd-shaped pieces of paper and backs of envelopes. If the data is suitable, and a computer is available, this is an excellent way of storing information which can easily be retrieved later.

Analysing the results

Analysing the information may need to be carried out by an expert, particularly if it has been gathered by one. But whoever it is done by, accuracy and objectivity are essential. It is very easy to leave out any information that upsets the pattern which seems to be emerging. It is also quite difficult to ignore the opinion of an interested person, for example the office manager who was asked why he had a high labour turnover. If, in the investigation, it emerged that eight people left for jobs with more pay, two because they moved out of the district when their husbands got new jobs, and one because she 'wanted a more interesting job', it is obvious that the reason for the high turnover resulted from something other than not-the-latest equipment, more probably from the comparatively low salaries paid by the company.

Deciding the conclusions

Analysing results inevitably leads to conclusions. These must be formulated with complete honesty: they may be what the originators of the report expected and wanted; they may be exactly the reverse. If it emerges, for example, that changing the layout of the factory would result in increased production, and that the trade unions involved would agree to this, then the conclusion is to go ahead. If, on the other hand, the trade unions would not agree to the changes, then management has a difficult decision to make. But in its negotiations it will have as ammunition the findings which are in the report. If the investigation shows that changing the factory layout would not significantly improve production, then it would be better to drop the whole idea, however dear to the heart of the production director it might be.

The report has to be written. At this stage it is essential to refer back to the mandate. For whom is the report to be written? Is it for one person or many? Is the level of understanding of the problem

the same for all who will read it and who will make decisions resulting from it? If it is for one person, there are fewer problems. If it is
for several people with varying degrees of knowledge and understanding, then the problems are increased. Devices must be invented
for making sure that the report is meaningful (as far as possible) to
all who will read it and make judgements about it. It must be taken
into account that all parts of a report are not equally important to
those who will consider it. The managing, production, finance and
personnel directors of a manufacturing company will all be interested in a report on the effects of reducing the amount of stock held
and increasing the number of times it is turned over in a year. The
managing director will be most interested in, and concerned about,
the total difference this would make to the overall running of the
factory. The production director will analyse very carefully what
problems would be revealed: delivery of components, work in progress, meeting customers' requirements. The finance director will
be working out the results of the more effective use of assets and the
reduction in borrowing. The personnel director will be imagining
the reaction of the workforce in general, and the shop stewards in
particular, to all the changes.

It is essential to write a preliminary draft of a report, and it should
be a prototype. Once a shape is produced, it is difficult to get away
from it. Therefore, before starting, the planning must be done. The
most important thing is to get firmly into the writer's mind the purpose of the report, and for whom it is written. It must supply the
information asked for if it has been commissioned, as is usually the
case. The writer and his opinions are immaterial; it is being written
for someone else.

Selecting supporting material

The data has been collected, it must now be selected. If the research
has been planned and carried out with the mandate always in view,
there should not be much material to throw out except trivia. It has
to be arranged, however, and arranged in a logical order rather than
the order in which it was obtained as this is probably the order in
which it will appear in the notes.

The interpretation of the data will have been made by the time it has been collected. Hypotheses will have been formulated as the facts were accumulated, and either rejected or accepted as more facts were gathered. After a mysterious plane crash from which there were no survivors to supply any information, the first hypothesis was that there had been a bomb on board which had exploded, causing the plane to break up in the air. As more and more wreckage was examined, this hypothesis was rejected in favour of metal corrosion as the cause of the crash. The report will give all the data and supply the evidence for the rejection of one hypothesis and the acceptance of another. Neither will be conclusive unless bomb damage or corroded metal is found.

Writing the report

Before beginning to write, structure and layout must be decided. A possible structure would be:

> statement of terms of reference
>
> summary
>
> contents
>
> main body of report
>
> conclusions
>
> appendices
>
> acknowledgements

The statement of the terms of reference must come first, so that any reader will know what it is all about. The summary should come next, although it will be written last, so that readers can easily take in the outline and see the structure. Also, very busy people who are not intimately involved can quickly get an overall view of the findings. The summary must give just the right amount of information to make these things possible. It is not necessary to write the body of the report twice, but neither should the summary be indistinguishable from the table of contents.

The table of contents, with page numbers, will enable readers to find their way about the report and, as its name implies, say what is in it. For those who want to go straight from the summary to the section which interests or concerns them most, the table of contents will tell them where to find it.

The main body of the report will give the data in a logical order. Decisions must be made as to how much information is in the report proper, and how many details are put into one or more appendices. Too many details obscure the main arguments of the report. This is a decision which is important, as not enough information makes the report unconvincing, and too much makes it less readable and certainly less memorable. Footnotes are an abomination and should be avoided at all costs, unless they are specifically required (i.e. by learned journals).

The conclusions must be stated as succinctly as possible, and should follow logically from the data in the report. No new material should be introduced at this stage. It should do as it says: conclude.

The appendices should contain detailed information, which readers may or may not want to read. They will probably read those things which interest them most.

It is common courtesy to acknowledge help that has been given in producing the report; and people like to know that their help has been appreciated.

When the first draft is written down, it can be checked, criticized and altered. It is much more effective to write a first draft and then look at it critically than it is to try to get it right first time. If it is possible, the first draft should be given to someone, whose opinion matters, for him to comment upon it. This may be one of the people who commissioned it; it may be someone in a similar position to the person who asked for it. What the writer wants and needs to find out is whether or not the report is communicating satisfactorily. Obviously if it is confidential or top secret, this cannot be done.

When the second, and hopefully last, draft is to be written, the details of layout must be decided. This is not for cosmetic reasons. The appearance of a report should be thought of as a way to communicate its contents to the best advantage. A well-laid-out report is certainly pleasing to look at but, more important, it is easy to read, it helps retention and can make reference easy.

Chapter divisions, headings, marginal headings, spacing, typefaces, indentations and tabulations must be used. The writer must think in terms of layout. Pages of unbroken text are off-putting, and variety can be achieved by layout. Bold marginal headings are extremely useful for easy reference, which the readers will appreciate.

Before writing the second draft, the first should be rigorously pruned. Nothing is more irritating to readers than repetition. Part of the process of putting the material into a logical order involves gathering together all the points and illustrations which belong to a particular subject and then getting these parts of the whole in an order which makes sense. There is no need to repeat the same things, unless it is definitely necessary to do so for a purpose.

The language of a report should be simple and straightforward. This does not mean that technical terms must be avoided, as many reports relate to a particular science and it would be ludicrous to try to avoid the associated terminology. It means that the structure of sentences should be simple: sub-clauses and other convoluted ways of saying things should be avoided.

In lengthy reports, some writers like to show the sub-divisions by a system of numbering. There are various conventions which use upper- and lower-case Roman numerals, Arabic numerals, upper- and lower-case letters, or a decimal system. For example:

II	2
II:a	2.1
II:ai	2.1.1
	2.1.2
	2.1.3

Whether this serves any useful purpose is doubtful. If the pages are numbered, the main headings stand out clearly, and paragraph headings are printed in bold in the margin, there is no difficulty in leading anyone to the place to which you wish to refer: 'On page 10 under the heading Reasons for Staff Leaving, paragraph Left District . . .' Government reports adopt the simple procedure of numbering the paragraphs consecutively. They can go up to many hundreds, but finding the place is no more difficult than finding number 903 in a hymn book.

There follows an extract from a report laid out in a way which makes it look pleasant, easy to read, and easy for reference.

Reducing Clerical Staff Turnover

TERMS OF REFERENCE

At the Board meeting of July 10 1985, the Personnel Director was asked to instruct the Office Manager to investigate reasons for the clerical staff turnover being twice as high as that of the rest of the employees, and to recommend action to combat this.

Clerical staff turnover investigation

SUMMARY

Records of all clerical staff appointed and leaving in the last five years were examined:
application forms
interview notes
letters of appointment
performance assessments
letters of resignation.

Staff records examined

The stated reasons for leaving were analysed and these were found to fall into 4 main categories.

Reasons for leaving established

Some reports need to be translated, for example those for a multi-national company. The same rules hold good as for translating instructions: the translator must be translating into his native language and be familiar with the subject of the report. Often the translation is more difficult than for instructions, as there will certainly be more narrative, and there cannot be so much reliance on illustrations.

15 On the Dotted Line

Forms and communication

A form is a question-and-answer communication technique. When information of the same kind from enough people is needed by a person or organization for a specific purpose, then a form comes into being. It is obvious that the first piece of information asked for will be a means of identifying the form-filler, usually name and address. Forms are generally printed, but the questions can equally well be on the visual display unit of a computer and the answers keyed in or written with a light-pen, and there are other electronic devices for showing questions and recording answers.

There is a series of stages involved in obtaining information by way of a form:

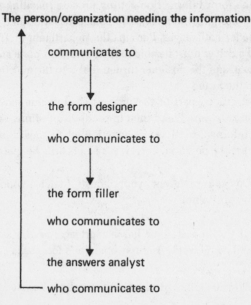

The person/organization needing the information

communicates to

the form designer

who communicates to

the form filler

who communicates to

the answers analyst

who communicates to

There is ample opportunity for communication to be less than good at each stage.

It has already been seen that deciding what information to *give* is difficult; do you remember 'Walk up one floor or down two for improved lift service'? It appears to be equally difficult to decide and communicate what information it is necessary to *obtain* for a particular purpose. The application form for obtaining a driving licence asks: 'Can you read letters and figures 3 inches high at a distance of 67 feet?' Not many form-fillers will be conscientious enough to set up an experiment to find out. They, correctly no doubt, interpret this question as 'can you read a car number plate at [what seems to them] a reasonable distance'. Incidentally, if the answer to this and similar questions is 'No', the licence will not be granted unless all the applicant wishes to drive is a mowing machine; and if the applicant is unscrupulous enough to lie, the form is valueless – so in either case it might as well be scrapped. One question to the applicant's doctor would be more reliable: 'In your opinion, is Mr Bloggs medically fit to drive a motor vehicle?'

This example shows that it is difficult to separate the first two stages of the form information-getting process (needing the information and desiging the form), and sometimes the same person is responsible for both stages. Perhaps the Department of Transport's rule is that a driver must be able to read a number plate at a reasonable distance, and the designer turned that into the question which appears on the form.

The most crucial part of the process is to decide exactly what information is required, and then to produce questions which will elicit that information. If an organization advancing money wants to know what the potential borrower's assets are, the question:

> Do you own/rent your house (delete whichever is inapplicable)

is useless if the householder has a mortgage, as the size of the mortgage will be relevant. A cruise operator's form asks

> Do you walk with the aid of crutches? Yes/No

The answer is 'Yes' if you have just broken your leg, but, all being well, will be 'No' by the time you sail.

Like other parts of the communication process, it is often thought that anyone of reasonable intelligence can design forms. That this is not so is indicated by such absurdities as providing half an inch of space in which to write an inch of information. This is an old joke, but the practice continues. A great deal of research has been done recently on the design of forms, and anyone embarking on this task should be well acquainted with what has been discovered.

There are a great many different kinds of questions. Some simply require a free response: name, address, telephone number. Others ask the form-filler to tick one selection among several:

Single Room	Twin Room	Double Room	Family Room

There are other types of multiple-choice questions:

Do you buy our paper:
every day   ☐
occasionally   ☐
Saturdays   ☐
on holiday   ☐
tick (√) the appropriate box

There are YES/NO questions with the instruction 'delete as required' or 'tick the appropriate answer'. As we have seen in the 'Do you own/rent your house' question, the answer may not be simply yes or no. The designers of forms should make everything as easy as possible for the form-fillers, particularly in making sure that the question is understood, and can be answered in the way specified.

Are you the householder?

If three families are living in one house, unless a clear and unambiguous definition of 'householder' is provided, this is a very difficult question to answer. Perhaps whatever is in the definition should be in the question, instead of 'householder'.

Few people actually enjoy filling in forms, and saving time is important, so ticking or ringing or putting a cross in, being quicker than writing, is to be recommended when it makes sense.

The overall appearance of a form can be intimidating. However long one has had a passport, the form to be filled in for renewal is the same as for first-time applicants. At the time of writing, it consists of four pages, plus four pages of notes, and an index card. The actual form to be filled in starts on the second page. Pages 2, 3 and 4 look alarming, but there is a clever algorithmic device (see Chapter 11) which makes the actual filling in simple, particularly for renewal, as the algorithm takes the filler-in past everything which is not relevant to his or her case. Had the front page been better designed, mainly to allay fears, it would be a very good form – although the relevance of the date of birth of a divorced woman's ex-husband is difficult to guess at.

The type of form with jumping procedures shown on page 177 is not common yet, but it is worth considering, particularly as it enables one form to be used for more than one situation, as in the passport form. This form has, as we have said, four pages of notes. These are helpful, and so is the checklist at the end of the form. When documents have to be sent with the form, such as birth, marriage or divorce certificates, plus a cheque, it is easy to leave one out, and then the whole procedure has to start again.

The four pages of notes show that the form is not self-explanatory. Another difficulty for form-fillers is that sometimes they do not know where to find the information asked for. Typical questions of this sort are:

What is your National Insurance number?

What is your hospital number?

What date did you join the company?

If a form asks for information which fillers have difficulty in finding, notes advising where it can be found are helpful and time-saving.

In companies, there is a tendency for forms to proliferate. One

TO BE FILLED IN BY ALL APPLICANTS   *Read note 6

Have you had any sort of passport before or applied for
any passport?   YES   NO
                                                        □   □

Is your last passport attached?   YES   NO
                                                        □   □

Previous passport number

                                        Please complete section 11

Is your husband/wife to be included on your passport? YES   NO
                                                        □   □

Have they had any sort of passport before?   YES   NO
                                                        □   □

Is their previous passport attached?   YES   NO
                                                        □   □

Previous passport number

                                        Please complete section 11

CAUTION
You are warned that the making of an untrue statement for the purpose of procuring a passport is a criminal offence. Passport Office procedures include a check on the authenticity of countersignatories. The application should not be countersigned until the form has been completed, signed and dated by the applicant.

fruit-importing company with £60 million sales, and with more than forty depots in England, had over fifty different forms which had to be filled in, in each depot. Some had to be dealt with daily, some weekly, some monthly, and some from time to time. It took five months to train someone to fill in these forms which were necessary for the branch accounting system. This is from the *Financial Times'* account of what was done to reduce training time and complexity:

> Over fifty accounting forms were grouped under headings like goods in, goods out, control, or staff. Then came the training reform. This took the shape of what in engineering terms is called templates – or in fact a series of ten form-filling guides. The trainee simply looks at a chart which tells him how to pick the appropriate colour-coded guide for whichever recording procedure he has to perform. He may have to deal with goods received for sale on commission, or credit control and lorry profitability, or transfer of fruit.
>
> The guide tells the trainee, and shows him in graphical form, what to enter where, whom to consult for additional information, even where to put a 'dash'.
>
> It could not be simpler. No doubt this method gives confidence to any green newcomer that he will be able to cope with what must seem to him to be a dauntingly complicated job. And he can learn without having anyone breathing down his neck.

Perhaps a rationalization of all the forms would have been a good idea to make sure that the same information was not asked for several times but, none the less, the company claimed that the job the consultants had done had reduced the training time from five months to one which, with so many depots, was a considerable saving in time and therefore money.

There are two lessons to be learnt from this story. The first is that the quantity of forms in any business should not be allowed simply to grow. When it is suggested that a new form is produced, it should first be considered whether an existing form can have additions or be changed to accommodate the new information required. The second is that the form-filler should be given as much help as he needs. As part of the exercise described, the form-filling guide had notes such as:

GET two blanks of Form CL25C and carbon.

Note: The form for this month may already have been part prepared with the Road Transport statistics entered.

To fill in this form

YOU NEED:
1. Special Cash Sheet CL8 for the month.
2. Summary of casual wages SF12 for the month.

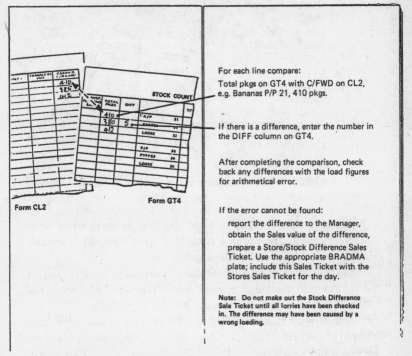

For each line compare:

Total pkgs on GT4 with C/FWD on CL2, e.g. Bananas P/P 21, 410 pkgs.

If there is a difference, enter the number in the DIFF column on GT4.

After completing the comparison, check back any differences with the load figures for arithmetical error.

If the error cannot be found:
report the difference to the Manager,
obtain the Sales value of the difference,
prepare a Store/Stock Difference Sales Ticket. Use the appropriate BRADMA plate; include this Sales Ticket with the Stores Sales Ticket for the day.

Note: Do not make out the Stock Difference Sale Ticket until all lorries have been checked in. The difference may have been caused by a wrong loading.

Form CL2   Form GT4

Employees soon get familiar with forms which have to be completed frequently. To begin with, guides are helpful, but they will soon be put on one side. Forms of any complexity which are filled in infrequently, need a guide to hand for use when the occasion arises.

Guides for form filling serve another purpose. New personnel can begin work with no training, and in these days of rapid labour turnover, this is a distinct advantage.

A useful device for helping form-fillers is a series of templates which fit over the forms and give precise guidance on what information should go where.

Each procedure was analysed and an aid was made to fit the form involved, using apertures to give precise guidance on what information should go into each box and in what form.

Training in this last case was not sensible, as some forms were used very rarely. The use of a computer made accuracy essential. The manual codified rather than instructed.

There are questions on forms which require a crystal ball to obtain the information needed to answer them: 'What is the replacement value of the total contents of your house?' If a crystal ball is not available, to work this out would take hours of time and an immense amount of research. 'What is today's price for the dinner service we got as a wedding present, and have added to since?' . . . 'Can we ask how much the desk is worth which your parents gave us?' Even worse is: 'What is replacement value of the unique item in your collection of porcelain?' By definition, something unique has no replacement value. Does this question really mean: 'What amount of money would compensate you for the loss of something irreplaceable?'

8

Identity mark or herd book number

If the number is changed, or a number is added, write in the complete correct number here. Enter it so that the last figure is in the last space, column 24. An oblique is one space.

Card * Code	Herd Number	Line	H.B. Att.	Identity Mark Reference No.		Current Calving Date	
Cols 1-2	3-10	11-13	14	15-24		25-30	
05						D M	Y

9

Type of number

Use this chart to decide what to enter in this space.

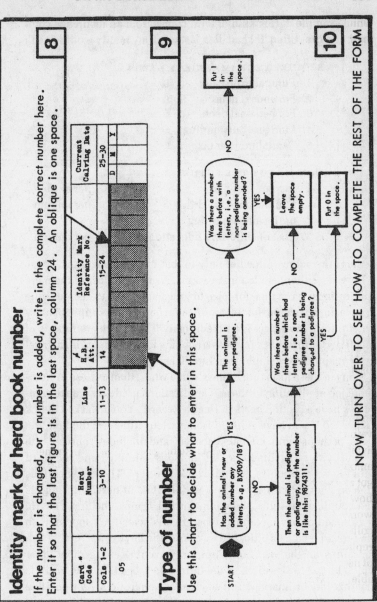

START

Has the animal's new or added number any letters, e.g. BX909/18?

— NO → Then the animal is pedigree or grading-up, and the number is like this: 9874311.

— YES → The animal is non-pedigree.

Then the animal is pedigree or grading-up, and the number is like this: 9874311.
→ Was there a number there before which had letters, i.e. a non-pedigree number is being changed to a pedigree?
— NO → Leave the space empty.
— YES → Put 0 in the space.

The animal is non-pedigree.
→ Was there a number there before with letters, i.e. a non-pedigree number is being amended?
— NO → Put 1 in the space.
— YES → Leave the space empty.

10

NOW TURN OVER TO SEE HOW TO COMPLETE THE REST OF THE FORM

A section of the performance aid incorporating all information needed by the scrutineer to do the job.

One example of this kind of form comes from an insurance company, and is entitled 'If I had died last week my family would need':

REQUIRED FOR IMMEDIATE NEEDS

1. Funeral expenses   £
2. For emergencies   £
3. For personal debts   £
4. Mortgage outstanding   £
5. Capital transfer tax   £

INCOME FOR THE FUTURE

1. Income for widow   £   per annum
2. Maintenance for children   £   per annum
   until self-supporting
3. Cost of children's education   £   per annum

Perhaps the value of this lies only in that it makes one think.

Nowadays there are too many forms. A great number of them are applications: for grants, for jobs, to join something, to get a driving licence, for a pension, for unemployment benefit, for supplementary benefit, for a mortgage, for a credit card. Then there are reports of accidents for insurance purposes, booking for a holiday with a travel agency, appraising employees, intelligence tests.

Many of these forms are useless, some worse than useless. A number of job application forms and applications to life assurance companies have a section headed 'Health Record'. You are asked to tick YES or NO if you have suffered from various illnesses; the first line deals perhaps with mental disorders and includes 'nerves', the second with other illnesses and includes 'fainting', and the third with digestive troubles, including 'indigestion'. The conscientious filler-in knows that he was in a terrible state of nerves during his first couple of air-raids, so he puts his tick against the first YES. He is ashamed of having fainted when he dislocated his shoulder, so the second YES gets a tick. His weakness is buying and eating fish and chips on the way home from any evening engagement, after which he has indigestion, so the third YES gets a tick. The result is that this very ordinary person emerges as a neurotic, with a possible heart condition and incipient gastric ulcers. Ridiculous? Maybe, but only a slight exaggeration.

Market research companies are great users of forms. They conduct surveys for the purpose of increasing their clients' sales. Questionnaires are given out at the end of holidays, for example, or to subscribers to magazines to discover what about the product is liked or disliked, and to collect suggestions for improvement. Most of the questions on these forms are multiple-choice, with boxes to tick.

Sometimes the researchers fill in the forms themselves, by calling at houses or stopping people in the street, and asking questions. The value of such surveys depends on three things: how good the questions are; how well they are analysed; what conclusions and recommendations result from the analyses.

Most of the research is published in papers in journals, but information about research on form design can be obtained from the Medical Research Council Applied Psychology Unit, 15 Chaucer Road, Cambridge CB2 2EF.

Those companies which produce forms should be aware of all the research which has been done, and take note of it. Above all, new forms should be tried out on a cross-section of the people who will have to fill them in. Then, any difficulties or ambiguities can be put right before the form is issued.

If the reader wishes to help in the reduction of the number of forms and the difficulty of filling them in, he should refuse to answer any question he does not fully understand or for which he does not know where to find the answer, and return the form uncompleted with a brief note of explanation.

To design a 'good' form, one writer on the subject has suggested that a team of experts is necessary: one in the subject matter, one in verbal communication, one in typographical design and one in the analysis of the answers to the questions. No doubt the result would be a camel-form.

16 Ladies and Gentlemen . . .

Communicating in presentations

A speech, a lecture, a talk, an illustrated talk, a presentation, all have this in common: they are performances and, like all performances, they need a great deal of preparation and rehearsal, so that they will appear completely effortless, although this is the last thing that they are.

The difference between them is difficult to define. Speeches and lectures are, on the whole, formal, and are made to large audiences. There is, perhaps, a take-it-or-leave-it attitude to the audience. Talks, illustrated talks and presentations are usually given to smaller audiences and, in business, for a specific purpose. This may be to present the annual report and accounts to the whole company; to introduce a company's new product to the sales force; to persuade the board that a profit-sharing scheme would be a good thing; to sell the company's products to potential customers; to explain a system of job-evaluation and appraisal to shop stewards . . . the possibilities are legion.

Standing in front of an audience, large or small, friendly, neutral or unfriendly, makes most people nervous. This can show by fidgeting in various ways, such as jingling coins in a pocket, waving one's hands around, walking about or constantly clearing the throat. This is not only a giveaway, but is highly distracting to the audience who, instead of listening to what is being said, begin to count the jingles or the waves or the coughs. Talking too fast is another sign of nerves; it makes what the speaker has to say difficult to listen to, and can make him finish ten minutes before the allotted time. 'Nerves' are inevitable, but if nervous manifestations can be avoided and that energy canalized into giving the presentation an 'edge', only good can result.

Yet another nervous sign is looking not at the audience but at some distant point in space. This removes the speaker from the audience, and he misses their reactions to what he is saying. If he deliberately focuses his eyes on different members of the audience in turn, they feel that they are being spoken to personally, and are more inclined to listen. He must, of course, avoid fixing his eyes on one hapless individual who will begin to wonder what is wrong with his appearance.

Inexperience leads a speaker to talk with his back to the audience, particularly when writing on a blackboard or flip chart, or pointing out things of interest on a picture or map. He is often afraid of not speaking for a few moments. If he is writing on a board or flip chart, the audience will be concentrating on watching what is being written, and speaking at the same time is unnecessary. This is one reason why nothing lengthy should be written up in the course of the presentation, but prepared in advance. Nothing can take the place of experience, but preparation and rehearsal can do a lot to help.

All presentations have the same aim, which is to sell something; this may be not an object, say an electric car, but a concept, such as market research, and to make the audience enthusiastic. The main causes of failure are not having enough information about the audience; the audience not identifying with the presenter; and not giving them the information which they need and want.

The presenter must find out as much as is possible about his audience. To begin with, why will they be there? Did he invite them? Did the boss make the arrangements for the presentation? Did the audience invite the presenter? These things are easy to find out. Is the presenter known to the audience and, if so, why? How many people will be there? What will the audience know about the subject? To be safe, if the last question cannot be answered, no knowledge should be assumed, but the presenter should be prepared to adjust very quickly if this is found to be wrong. If possible, the likely attitude of the audience should be discovered. Shop stewards may not be particularly receptive to a new system of job evaluation, or the whole workforce to relocation; but management of a manufacturing company will probably welcome a new method of stock control which will save a great deal of money, and the directors of a chain of retail stores will certainly be interested in a device for avoiding till losses.

The presenter may have no control over where he is to give his presentation. It may have to be in the boardroom or the canteen, in which case he has to do the best he can. Where he has a choice, there are important factors to be considered. It is very irritating if the meeting place is difficult to find, or there are no parking facilities. Adequate directions must be given to those planning to attend. The hall or room must be suitable for that particular presentation; six people in a ballroom will feel uncomfortable. There must be the right number of seats, and they must be comfortable. Heating and ventilation must be checked. If electrical equipment is being used, sockets must be located; it must be decided whether an extension lead is necessary. The audience must be provided with paper, pencils and hand-outs. Everything must be checked well in advance. In spite of this, as Murphy has told us, 'If it can go wrong, it will go wrong.' Any equipment being used must be checked before the presentation begins. The fact that it was all right last time it was used doesn't matter; it can be upset on the journey. Spare bulbs and any other small replacement parts are essential. So is a torch. Audio-visual equipment going wrong can ruin a presentation if potential disaster has not been prepared for and some way of doing without selected.

Preparing the actual presentation involves first collecting information, and then making a double selection. As much material as is available should be collected; then that which is to be used in the presentation should be put on one side; next, that which should be kept for amplification or for answering questions should be noted; and lastly, the rest should be discarded. The selection will be dictated by the aim of the presentation and the presenter's knowledge of his audience. He must assess how much information to give, and in what degree of detail. Evidence must always be produced to support any statement. Statistics are useful; they need not be given in the presentation, but someone will want to know the exact time or number or saving.

Any talk, short or long, formal or informal, should have a shape. There must be a beginning, a middle and an end. A useful guide is that the beginning should state what is going to be said, and grab the interest of the audience; the end should summarize what has been said and drive home the main points; and the middle should be a logically structured exposition of the information.

Tell them what you're going to tell them.

Then tell them.

Then tell them what you've told them.

It is a sign of failure if the presenter has to admit that he has left out a vital piece of information, or if a question shows this to have been the case.

What of that middle bit, the meat of the presentation? It has been said that it should be 'logically structured'. There are various ways of doing this. For example, for presenting a new company product to salesmen:

what it is

what it does

how it does it

why people should buy it

why it is better than other similar products

how much it costs

would be a sensible structure. A chronological structure could be used for a presentation to those employees involved in relocation: what has happened over the years to make this necessary.

Part of the preparation must include deciding what visual aids will be used. These, properly used, add a great deal to the interest of the presentation. They make a change from the presenter's voice, and one picture /chart / diagram / map can often say more than many words. What will be used depends on what is available, what can be made available, the subject, the size and composition of the audience, the room where the presentation is to be made, and the budget. Everyone must be able to see, without difficulty, anything which is to be shown. This must be tested in the actual room, or one of similar size and shape. A long narrow room presents problems which one of the same area, but square, does not.

Chalkboards and flip charts are old-hat – but they are cheap, can be used very effectively to create and hold audience interest, are completely flexible, and are not to be despised for small or medium-sized audiences.

Overhead projectors are often rejected in favour of more sophisticated electronic equipment; but again, transparencies are cheap and easy to produce, they can be used to structure a presentation so that the presenter cannot go wrong, and for small or medium-sized audiences they are hard to beat.

Slides can be very beautiful, but they are difficult to handle, get out of order, and nothing can spoil a presentation more effectively than dropping them all just after it has begun.

Slide-tape programmes can be extremely effective, although there is no flexibility, and if the slides get out of order in any way, the whole presentation is ruined. These programmes can easily be put on video cassettes, so, if the equipment is available, the difficulties can be overcome.

Films, and films on video cassettes, are very expensive, although they can be very good indeed, and can be shown to large audiences. A large screen can be used in place of the ordinary television screen.

It is, of course, sometimes possible to show the actual object one is presenting. If the audience is small enough for everyone to see or, better still, try it out, this is admirable, but if one person is playing with a microcomputer while the rest just sit longing to have a go, the result will be boredom and consequent disaster.

However well the presenter has collected and selected his material, structured his talk, and chosen his visual aids, he can still spoil it all. His audience expects to be interested as well as informed, even entertained. From the moment he appears, his audience is sizing him up. He must fit in with their expectations. Correct business clothes must be worn. If the weather is hot, someone in authority, perhaps the chairman, or the presenter himself, may suggest that jackets may be removed. Business women have no stereotyped dress to match the business suit, but they have their own conventions.

The speaker's voice is his most important tool. He must learn to speak clearly, to project his voice, and to vary its pitch and volume. This will help keep his audience's interest. It is necessary for most people to practise speaking in public, and although practice does not make perfect, it certainly improves performance. Microphones are a trap for the unwary. Practice in using them is absolutely essential. However distraught he may feel inside, he must show a calm and confident exterior, and deliberately refrain from those signs of nerves, jingling and waving and walking and clearing his throat.

The moment arrives: he is about to begin. Sometimes, if the presentation is reasonably informal, he will have to stop people from drinking their coffee and gossiping, and indicate that they must get to their places and listen to him. This must be done with authority; he must be both seen and heard. It is said that it is better to drop or knock over something heavy to attract attention rather than to wait drearily to be noticed. Sometimes one is formally introduced by a chairman. This can be a mixed blessing: he sometimes tells the audience what he thinks the presenter is going to say. It is difficult to know which is worse: whether he is right or wrong. If he is right, the wind has largely been taken out of the presenter's sails. If he is wrong, there is the embarrassing job of putting him right.

One way or another, the presentation has to start, and the relationship with the audience has to be established. The first golden rule is not just to read what is to be said. First and foremost it separates the reader from the audience. He can't make eye-contact with them, which is a valuable way of establishing a relationship, and he can't see their reactions. Reading a script also makes it difficult to change what is to be said. Above everything else, reading sounds different from talking. Professionals can read and make it sound like ordinary speaking, but amateurs can't. One way of establishing a rapport with the audience is to get them to identify with the speaker: 'We are all engineers of some sort' . . . 'I imagine we all got held up on the M6 this morning' . . . 'I would like to take my jacket off, please do the same'.

A recognized way of getting an audience to feel happy with the speaker is for him to make them laugh. Sadly, this has led to the telling of totally irrelevant jokes, often in doubtful taste, at the beginning of any kind of talk. If the speaker has something really funny to say which is relevant to the presentation, there is no better way of beginning. Another useful device is to start with things everyone can agree with. This can simply be a matter of phraseology: 'I am suggesting that the PR921 may be of use to you, but only you can decide if it will.'

Getting attention is one thing, keeping it is another. If the structure of a presentation is obvious, so that the audience is aware of where it is going, that is part of the battle. It is also a good idea to involve individuals in the audience. If what someone has said is referred to, or some work or product of an audience member's company is mentioned, interest is revived. Variety is helpful, and the sensibly spaced use of visual aids prevents boredom. It has been experimentally established that span of attention is very short, and this should be remembered when planning a presentation.

Perhaps the most devastating thing to happen when talking in public is to dry up. It may be because the mind goes a complete blank; it may be because the material has run out quicker than was expected. It has been suggested that reading from a script is not a good idea. None the less, it is advisable to write out in full what is to be said, and to say it into a tape-recorder. In this way the talk can be timed reasonably accurately, and the speaker can hear what he sounds like and practise until he cuts out the 'ers' and 'ums', and gets away from the exact words of his script. When writing, it is difficult to be colloquial, and to add those thoughts here and there which make it all sound spontaneous.

After this, the speaker should prepare his own prompts. If he is totally familiar with the material, which he should be, then main point headings should be enough to keep him going. These should be written large enough for him to see without having to pick up papers, and without peering. Overhead-projector transparencies are extremely useful as prompts, and they can structure a whole presentation so that by showing them the presenter can't lose the thread of his talk.

Running out of material will be avoided if the talk has been timed accurately with a tape-recorder as part of the preparation, but a little allowance should be made for talking faster because of nerves. Additional material should also be provided, which can be used if the presentation proper ends too soon. This must be carefully chosen so that it doesn't appear to be merely a time-filler.

The summary is what people will remember best, so it must be carefully prepared and absolutely clear. It is advisable to give the audience something to take away, and included in this should be a copy of the summary.

At the end of most talks and presentations, a time is allowed for questions and answers. These can be daunting. Perhaps the worst to deal with are those which aren't questions at all, but are spurious additions to what has been said, made by someone who wants to show off and show up the speaker's deficiencies. The only way to deal with these is to spot them at once, and make an arrangement to have a discussion after the presentation is over. Sometimes someone in the audience can give genuine additional information which the speaker doesn't know. In this case, he should be listened to and thanked. Then there are questions which show that the speaker has been misunderstood. If it is his fault, he should put the questioner right and apologize for causing misunderstanding. If it is the questioner's fault, then he must tactfully be put right.

The speaker should be prepared for that devastating silence when 'Any questions' is asked. It may mean that the presentation has been so complete that no one in the audience can think of anything to ask. It may be that the audience is not enthusiastic enough to want to know anything more. In either case, this is the speaker's last chance. He should have something prepared: 'I would like to know your views on . . .'; 'Has anyone any evidence to support / contradict what I have suggested . . .' Somehow, he must get people talking.

A presentation is an excellent chance for communication. It must not be wasted. Because of this, training in giving presentations should be given by every company, large or small. One multinational company known to the author trains all senior personnel from the chairman to the managers of small subsidiaries, and all its sales staff from the director to the people 'on the road'. These presentation training courses have become very popular, and improvements in the presentations given have been spectacular.

A suggested course would contain the following subjects:

eye focus

controlling the release of nervous energy

the use of visual aids

preparing visual aids: slides, tapes, overhead-projector transparencies

assessing the audience

audience expectations: the venue, the presenter's image

collecting and selecting information

preparing the presentation

getting and keeping the audience's attention

voice and the use of a microphone

dealing with questions

Murphy's law: be prepared

something to take away

Members of such a course should be asked to prepare and give two-minute, five-minute and fifteen-minute presentations. Closed-circuit television is an invaluable aid to such a course, as afterwards people can not only see themselves performing but, even more revealing and often devastating, see the audience's reactions.

Introducing a presenter has already been mentioned. Whoever does this job must know all that is necessary to interest the audience about him, and the information must be accurate and up to date. To introduce someone as Sales Manager when he has just been promoted to Marketing Director is unforgivable. Not to know that he has just been knighted for his services to industry, and to call him Mr Robinson instead of Sir Henry, is equally reprehensible. The story about the speaker who, after being introduced, started his talk by saying, 'After the chairman's introduction, I can hardly wait to hear what I'm going to say,' is an old chestnut. It's worth repeating because of its implicit warning: 'Don't overdo it.' Most important is to say something about the speaker which will make the audience feel that he is worth listening to. It is then up to him.

To thank someone for his presentation involves listening very carefully to everything he says, to the questions and comments of the audience, and to sum it all up as graciously as possible, and in very few words. No one wants to hear a repeat performance from the person delegated to give the vote of thanks.

Not everyone can be a star performer, but everyone can achieve a reasonable level of performance if the rules are obeyed.

17 *Still, Why Bother?*

What good communication brings with it

The reader will have noticed, and perhaps regarded it as an important omission, that there is nothing in this book about 'correct English'. A split infinitive has been mentioned once; the difference between 'ordinary' and 'posh' talk has been discussed; the drawbacks of long and involved sentences have been illustrated; but of grammar and syntax there is nothing. This is not because correct English is regarded as unimportant. The reason it has been left out is that there are excellent books on communication in general, and on business communication, which deal largely with how to write comprehensible correct English. That this is necessary is illustrated by reading a sample of letters received in almost any office. There is no need to do again here what has already been well done.

It was pointed out in Chapter 3 that 'Please walk up one floor or down two for improved lift service' cannot be faulted as an example of correct English, but it fails completely to communicate the message its writer intended. This book has been concerned with the wider and, in the author's opinion, more important subject: how to transfer information satisfactorily.

Language is still the most important medium for conveying information, although reading and writing it are becoming less necessary with the advance of audio-visual technology. Not everyone today will agree that a great deal is missed by not being able to read and write, except that it makes it impossible to fill in forms unaided.

The sheer complexity of modern life makes the ability to communicate essential, not least in business. Misunderstandings are extremely expensive in money, in time, in energy, and in strain.

In essence, what this book is asking its readers to do is to sort out what is to be communicated and get this information in the right order; to make sure what the result of the communication is intended to be; and to decide on the best way of achieving this result.

Language will usually be involved – although not necessarily so if the message is simple. Some of the accepted road-signs are good examples: *Senso unico* may not be understood, and it does not tell you which way it is permitted to drive; but the No Entry sign makes the situation clear. The language must fit the level of knowledge and the vocabulary of the recipients of the message. Jargon and technical terms may be used only between people who understand them. Sometimes, to avoid tedious circumlocutions, a glossary of unfamiliar words and phrases can go before, but not after, a communication.

To get the information in the right order seems simple enough, but it is not often achieved. If a vital stage in installing a washing machine is to turn off the water, this should come first, not after the kitchen has been flooded by someone following the installation manual. 'Before this can be done' comes half-way through the instructions for removing the covers of a typewriter on page 46 of this book. When a correct sequence has been found, it should be tried out by someone unfamiliar with the process.

The purpose of a communication is often wrongly assessed. There is a great difference between knowing how something works, and knowing how to operate it, yet many writers of user manuals mix up these two things. What is the purpose of explaining a pension scheme? Some people will say that it is so that a member will 'understand' how the scheme works. Really, it is so that he can work out his pension entitlement and other benefits, and account for the fact that five per cent is deducted from his salary. To explain a job-evaluation scheme adequately is to enable Joe to work out why, and therefore accept the fact that, Bill earns a little more than he does. The purpose of explaining the economic 'facts of life' is so that employees can be misled by neither management nor trade union, but assess situations for themselves with at least a certain amount of relevant information.

To select the correct medium for the message demands some thought. There is a tendency to choose a video programme because it is the 'in thing', rather than because it is the best way to communicate a particular piece of information. Audio-visual programmes are usually interesting and effective, but they only leave behind what is in the memory – unless there is something to take away as well. Charts, diagrams and pictures can replace, or add to, words.

To most people, the ability to communicate does not come naturally and at the time when it is needed. Training, trial-and-error learning and above all, discipline are necessary. It is in the discipline part of this that the pay-off comes. If, in the course of communicating in business, someone is trained, and trains himself, to sort things out logically, which is what 'in the right order' amounts to, he is unlikely to abandon this process either in other parts of his work or in his ordinary daily life . . . He might even be able to teach his wife to drive a motor car without the usual kerfuffle.

Afterword:
Office of the Future

by Rodney Dale and Tracy Stoten,
Business Literature Services Ltd, Cambridge

     A buzz-phrase which has been around for a year or two is the 'office of the future' or 'electronic office'. This conjures up various images which almost certainly include a television screen and computer keyboard as hardware and perhaps the idea that one can communicate via some network with everybody else in one's building, or in other parts of one's company, or perhaps anywhere in the world. Your vague image may well extend to some kind of *Star Trek* console from which a large number of diverse activities are controlled – perhaps world wide. Presumably in your daydream you have cast yourself in a top managerial position, and may even be driving these millions of pounds' worth of sophisticated equipment by means of voice commands.

     What is the reality? There are several drawbacks to the essentials of this office of the mind, a false creation, proceeding from the heat-oppressed brain. The first is that an all-singing, all-dancing set-up costs a great deal of money, and there's no point in my getting one if nobody else has got one. Of course this argument has been applied to all means of communication in their turn: talking is no use if there's no one to listen; sending morse is no good if there's no one to receive; having a telephone is no good if you're the only subscriber . . . and so on. If no one ever took a chance, there would never be any progress. But the higher the investment in the equipment, the fewer people there will be who are prepared to take the plunge and be first.

     'However,' you say, 'lots of people do have desktop computers, and are connected to the phone network and so on. Isn't that a good start?' Well, it is and it isn't. The main problem is that there are so many different standards; transferring data from one machine to another is not just a question of connecting a couple of wires. As long as there is a battle for standards (broad gauge versus narrow gauge; VHS versus Betamax) a large number of potential customers will be discouraged; and of those who take the chance, a lot will find that they have made the wrong choice.

Perhaps, in the context of the present work – communication – it is more profitable to look at the electronically based aids that one might reasonably expect to come across in a reasonably well-equipped office of the present than to speculate on the office of the future.

The typewriter

The typewriter has been around for so long now that it's easily overlooked. In the light of modern science you may well see it as an endangered species, but the typewriter still has a lot going for it. It's inexpensive, requires little maintenance, is instantly accessible, and portable. A typewriter is easily moved from one desk to another, from work to home and back again. And anyone can use it. Electrically or manually operated, they're virtually self-explanatory: load the paper, strike the key, the symbol's there on the page – and there's a wide choice of symbols and styles. And if it's really urgent, crucially important, the MD himself can tap it out and get it in the post. The designers haven't abandoned typewriters yet, either; constant improvements mean that many of the computer's memory and edit functions can be 'borrowed' without losing any of the small-machine benefits. No matter what elaborate equipment an office may boast, it will always be quicker and easier to rush through the odd address label or compliments slip on the typewriter.

The photocopier

Duplicating reams of paper is no longer the messy business it used to be. Even carbon copies are becoming obsolescent as photocopiers take more and more in their stride. Quick and easy to operate, they can reproduce single sheets or tackle more advanced tasks such as size reduction, enlargement, multiple and double-sided printing and collating – and even colour copying. Still, perhaps, not the most reliable item in the office, the problem's somewhat alleviated by the intelligent photocopier which diagnoses its own faults: if it wants you to call in the engineer, at least you won't have to waste time searching for jammed paper or topping up the toner.

The telephone

The telephone system is the largest in the world. Pick up a telephone and you can, theoretically, get in touch with any other telephone in the world. The telephone has been with us for over a century, during which it has developed from a few instruments in a local area, interconnected manually, to the sophisticated, automated, universal network of today. Now the telephone itself may be push-button operated, store numbers, tell the time, tell callers where you are when you're away, and when you'll be back. A private local exchange offers a similar host of useful features, and the public network and exchanges are being adapted to transmit everything digitally – essential for the electronic data society. Perhaps the most significant advance is the introduction of control by software (computer program) rather than by hardware (switches). But you'll still find *Homo technologicus* endeavouring to assert his mastery by using the telephone to call for a cup of coffee, and ending up going and making it himself.

The telephone answering machine

For some reason or other, a large number of people dry up when faced with the prospect of talking to a TAM. Both ends of the line can help combat this. The person preparing the message tape, realizing that many people will be put off by being answered by a machine – and yet, oddly enough, always prepared to listen to the message – could well incorporate a helpful guide, such as an alternative number to ring, or an indication of what time the phone will be manned again. It goes without saying (doesn't it?) that if you have a TAM you should remember to switch it on when you leave, that you should listen to it when you return, and that you should follow up any messages on it with all speed.

If you are the caller you will know from the sound of the phone being 'answered' that you are about to hear from a machine. You will know that in all probability it will utter a standard message, ending with a request that you 'speak after the tone'. Secure in the knowledge that this is going to happen, you can stop listening to the message and compose yourself to tell the machine who you are, who you're calling, why, and what you want the machine's owner to do (ring you back or whatever). If it is important that you leave the message, but you are still wrong-footed, you can always ring off, jot down a few notes, and ring the machine again. It's not a bad thing to tell the machine the time and date on which you called. The part of the exercise we have not quite mastered satisfactorily yet is how to say 'goodbye'; the growing convention seems to be to sing 'Byeeee' . . . listening to your messages is all part of the fun.

The dictating machine

Some people are affected by dictating machines as others are by telephone answering machines. People who could perfectly easily issue a clear instruction orally, or jot it down on a piece of paper, are overcome with embarrassment when faced with a microphone. It is, perhaps, rather like writers' block – faced with a sheet of paper, one's pen refuses to make a mark. We think that this is because they somehow feel that, once a word has been committed to paper, it is immutable. 'If you can't get it right, don't write it', seems to be the maxim, rather than 'Don't get it right, get it written'. Dictation is an art, and one well worth acquiring; it requires far fewer skills than learning to use a typewriter. And if you have the opportunity to correct what you have dictated, what have you to lose?

The first draft of this was dictated driving along in the car; it may not have been quite right the first time around, but at least it captured the gist of the writer's thoughts.

A hint for dictators: do accompany your tape with a note to help the transcriber. If you forget to issue such instructions as what paper to type it on, how you want it spaced out and so on, it is not much use dictating them on to the end of the tape. Even the innocuous 'all that's in capital letters, by the way' means tearing out the page and starting again. Unless of course, the transcriber is using . . .

The word processor

One of the most significant pieces of equipment in the modern office is the word processor. They come in various forms – the two great phyla are 'dedicated' word processors (which won't do anything else but process words) and computers with word-processing programs (which can fulfil a number of other computerly functions as well). Whatever the 'hardware' (that's the bit that hurts you if you kick it), the principles of word processing are the same; you type in text using a normal keyboard, with the chance of observing it on some sort of display as you do so. You can store the text, or you can print it out. You can edit it as you go along, or retrieve it from the store and edit it or print it out later. At its simplest, the function of editing entails correcting spelling mistakes, adding and deleting words and so on. The next level of facility (very useful) is to be able to rearrange blocks of text. More esoteric still is the possibility of asking the word processor to search for certain groups of characters – and even to change them to other groups if you wish; for example, if you are writing a novel and wish to change the name of your central character from Stan to Charlie, the word processor could be asked to perform this chore while you go for your coffee break.

Not only is all this possible, but the number of lines per page, the length of the lines, the spacing, the pagination and so on may all be set and changed as desired.

All these facilities add a new dimension to the arts of dictation and typing. The dictator can have afterthoughts about insertions or transpositions which in former times would drive the typist up the wall. He – or she – can dictate drafts while driving (or, when that's illegal, while being driven) and edit them later. Existing documents can be updated by changing names, dates, quantities and other details. Standing letters can be churned out over and over again. Leases, contracts, conditions of sale – and any other document you can think of which is basically the same from one edition to the next, with merely a change of detail – can be churned out at will.

Most serious word processors store the text on disc (or disk). Provided that everyone in the office is using the same sort of machine, it will be possible to transfer discs from one to another. Thus typists can take up and put down work and exchange it one with another as convenient. Discs can be sent from one place to another. Data can be sent from one machine to another via the telephone network. But all this depends on intercompatibility which, as we saw above, may be the Scylla on which the office of the future will founder.

Telex, fax and Teletext

If you have an urgent message to deliver to somebody in another building, you'll probably reach for the phone without a second thought. If you're lucky, you'll get a line, make the connection, and British Telecom will start totting up the bill. But suppose the person you want to contact is in New York. Getting put through to him a couple of times a week – always assuming he's there – can start to cost a small fortune. Likewise, repeatedly dictating long and complicated instructions to somebody just across town all weighs heavily on the budget, and is prone to error sooner or later. This is when you'll start to consider telex. For a fraction of the cost, you'll be able to send messages anywhere in the world. You'll still want to keep them short and to the point, so the saving will be even greater. So how does it work?

All you do is to dial the recipient from your telex machine and, when you're connected, you either type in your message or run a prepared tape through. It's received at the other end simultaneously and, all being well, passed on to the relevant person. It's amazing what authority and urgency are attached to a telex message; it can make people jump about as no phone call or letter can – a powerful sales aid, used properly.

Telex-receiving agencies have sprung up in most towns, so if you don't think your business warrants a machine of its own, you can join the books of a local bureau, let them send and receive your messages, and no one will be any the wiser.

Facsimile

So far so good. But as 'a picture is worth a thousand words', wouldn't it be good to be able to transmit pictures, diagrams and so on? Fax allows you to send copies of anything to anyone with a similar machine; the only disadvantage is, you can't be sure that anybody at the other end has noticed it's arrived.

The desktop / pocket calculator

The calculator is one gadget that has really caught on. We all use them – for adding up household bills, working out VAT, estimating how much tax we'll pay next month – and certainly in the office for estimating, pricing, timesheets, percentages and more scientific calculations. Strange to think there were those who insisted a slide-rule would do . . . The thing to beware of is losing the feel for 'order of magnitude' (where should the decimal point be?) and the facility for knowing instantly that $9 \times 8 = 72$, to name but one.

The computer

The computer is a much misunderstood beast – although, with the spread of home computers, it may be losing some of its mystique. On the other hand, since most home computers are used for playing games, this in itself may have given the computer an undeserved image. The other misconceptions about computers are that you have to be able to program them to be able to use them, and that you use them for 'doing sums'. They can certainly be used for 'doing sums', but they can be used for a lot of other things as well, and you certainly don't have to know about programming; a lot of people have spent a great deal of time writing programs for you – one such enables you to use your computer as a word processor without knowing anything at all about computing.

Another program which can be very useful is the 'spreadsheet'. This does have some element of 'doing sums' in it, but it does them for you and enables you to produce accounts and forecasts, typing different 'scenarios' and answering 'what if?' questions, as the jargon has it, without recourse to Tipp-Ex or erasers. If you have a spread-sheet program which is compatible with your word processing pro-gram, you will be able to merge information from the two and produce documents which contain both words and financial or stat-istical tables. A database program in the same suite (i.e. also compat-ible) will enable you, say, to call up information about different customers, incorporate it into the word-processed material, and give the impression that it has been prepared specially for them – though fewer people are fooled by that nowadays.

Teletext and video

While we're looking at screens, we should note that a wide variety of information is available via the (appropriately appointed) television set. The BBC transmits Ceefax (see facts – ouch!); ITV competes with its Oracle (Optional Reception of Announcements by Coded Line Electronics); British Telecom runs Prestel; there are other specialist database services. Many a boardroom now boasts a television set for important information on world stock markets, showing company videos, and watching Wimbledon, Test matches, etc.

Paper v. screens

One of the oft-cited excitements of the future is the idea that we shall have the paperless office; that all messages will be typed on keyboards and read on screens; that books will be replaced by plug-in chips containing an encyclopedic amount of information.

Electronic mail is here already, but using it seems to us to be somewhat tedious compared with the ease of looking through a pile of messages on paper – and they could be telex or fax messages.

To our mind, we are a long way from even a minor acceptance of the paperless office, and are unlikely to get much closer unless mankind becomes attuned to a radically different way of using paper and referring to books.

Paper and books are so easy to read on the train, to scribble notes on . . . and not everyone can use a keyboard anyway, though we would recommend it as a skill everyone should acquire. But think about the way we use reference books (not the same as reading a work of fiction from cover to cover). Really, it just isn't practical to have to plug into a machine in order to 'access' the information we personally find interesting. It's much *easier* to skim through an index or book and happen across something that catches your eye.

Ultimately, reading is a pleasure. A future in which we'll have to learn to operate (not to mention afford) a complex piece of machinery just to while away a winter's evening contentedly seems, happily, a long way off. Beside, what can beat the smell, look, feel – and the expectancy – of an unread book?

FOR THE BEST IN PAPERBACKS, LOOK FOR THE

In every corner of the world, on every subject under the sun, Penguin represents quality and variety – the very best in publishing today.

For complete information about books available from Penguin – including Pelicans, Puffins, Peregrines and Penguin Classics – and how to order them, write to us at the appropriate address below. Please note that for copyright reasons the selection of books varies from country to country.

In the United Kingdom: For a complete list of books available from Penguin in the U.K., please write to *Dept E.P., Penguin Books Ltd, Harmondsworth, Middlesex, UB7 0DA*

In the United States: For a complete list of books available from Penguin in the U.S., please write to *Dept BA, Penguin, 299 Murray Hill Parkway, East Rutherford, New Jersey 07073*

In Canada: For a complete list of books available from Penguin in Canada, please write to *Penguin Books Canada Ltd, 2801 John Street, Markham, Ontario L3R 1B4*

In Australia: For a complete list of books available from Penguin in Australia, please write to the *Marketing Department, Penguin Books Australia Ltd, P.O. Box 257, Ringwood, Victoria 3134*

In New Zealand: For a complete list of books available from Penguin in New Zealand, please write to the *Marketing Department, Penguin Books (NZ) Ltd, Private Bag, Takapuna, Auckland 9*

In India: For a complete list of books available from Penguin, please write to *Penguin Overseas Ltd, 706 Eros Apartments, 56 Nehru Place, New Delhi, 110019*

In Holland: For a complete list of books available from Penguin in Holland, please write to *Penguin Books Nederland B.V., Postbus 195, NL–1380AD Weesp, Netherlands*

In Germany: For a complete list of books available from Penguin, please write to *Penguin Books Ltd, Friedrichstrasse 10 – 12, D–6000 Frankfurt Main 1, Federal Republic of Germany*

In Spain: For a complete list of books available from Penguin in Spain, please write to *Longman Penguin España, Calle San Nicolas 15, E–28013 Madrid, Spain*